The XBRL Book

Simple, Precise, Technical.

by Ghislain Fourny

February 12, 2018

The XBRL Book by Ghislain Fourny

http://ghislainfourny.github.io/the-xbrl-book/

Revision history for the Second Edition
2018-02-10 First Release

ISBN 978-1979990721

Trademarks:
XBRL is a registered trademark of XBRL International, Inc. XML, XML Schema, XLink and XML Base are recommendations by the World Wide Web Consortium (W3C). All other trademarks are the properties of their respective owners.

Example data:
A lot of the examples of this book are largely inspired by the samples by Charles Hoffman, CPA, which he kindly provides as public domain. Some other examples are taken from fiscal filings publicly submitted to the SEC via the EDGAR system.

Intellectual Property Status of the XBRL specifications:
XBRL International requires educational content that explains XBRL to include the following paragraph referring to the XBRL specifications.

Contents

Chapter 1

Introduction

1.1 Why this book?

XBRL is currently gaining increasing acceptance worldwide, as reporting authorities encourage or require companies or banks to submit their reports in this format. There is a reason for this: data submitted as XBRL filings, that is, where each value or piece of information is tagged with its meaning and context, can be processed automatically by machines.

As a result, an ecosystem of tools and vendors has emerged, and people from all backgrounds — IT, Business, Finance, ... — are working together to further establish and grow this technology.

When I began to dive into the XBRL world, a few years ago, I searched for books on the matter. I quickly realized that, as a technical person with a scientific background, I could not find any that would explain XBRL at the appropriate level of abstraction: almost all books — for excellent reasons, it has to be said — focus on the business aspects of XBRL, and how to use it best within a company. They thus stick to high-level technical explanations. I ended up spending most of my time reading the XBRL specifications directly. I could also exchange emails with Charlie Hoffman, to whom I am extremely grateful for his insights, vision and patience.

Later, I did finally find a few more books that go into deeper technical details, however they do so at the level of the XML and XML Schema syntaxes rather than at the higher semantic level of XBRL itself. Of course, this is very useful for XML-savvy people to get started, but after a few years working with this technology, I became more and more conscious that understanding XBRL in terms of XML is a bit like learning C++ or Java in terms of the assembly code they produce.

Put simply, this book is the simple and precise starting point I wish I had had when I first encountered XBRL. Most of these pages do not require any XML or XML Schema knowledge, except for the one section in each chapter that goes into details about the syntax — but the latter can easily be skipped on a first read.

1.2 Business reporting today

Among the various software technologies that have been designed in the era of computers, there is one in particular that enjoys undisputed popularity among business users, from financial analysts to executives, through consultants and business analysts: spreadsheets.

While spreadsheets support some automation with the popular VBA scripts, they lack the ability to express their content in a standardized way that computers could understand and act on without human intervention.

XBRL solves this problem. Fiscal reports can be submitted to, say, the SEC in a uniform and standardized way, enabling financial analysts to create their reports on the fly and automatically. Moreover, it is easier than ever to validate the data filed to SEC and eliminate accounting mistakes, leading to reports of higher and higher quality every year. As of October 2015, Charlie Hoffman reported that two XBRL editors already reached the 90% correctness threshold — meaning that 90% of their XBRL filings showed no error for the validation criteria used, such as the fact that assets must match liability and equity.

1.3 Instances and taxonomies

The data in XBRL is submitted in a so-called XBRL instance. An XBRL instance contains facts. Each fact is a value that is tagged with a context that describes what it is about.

Instances are never submitted alone. They are submitted along with a taxonomy that gives meta-information about the contexts used in the reported facts. This part of XBRL is also known as a DTS (Discoverable Taxonomy Set).

Taxonomies can be created by reporting authorities so that companies can create their reports in a homogeneous way, but taxonomies can also be extended by them to fit their individual needs.

Taxonomies include formulas and validation rules that check that the submitted data is sound. They also organize the metadata in a structured way, just like a fiscal report on paper is structured and presented for being read by an investor.

1.4 Misconceptions about XBRL

We will start our journey through XBRL shortly. But first, let us go through some statements about XBRL that are commonly assumed, but I think are not right.

1.4.1 XBRL is XML

Yes, and no. Actually, no.

XBRL does use the XML syntax, which you will see if you open it with a text editor. But the same applies to an Excel (.xlsx) file: rename it as .zip and open it, and you will find XML. Yet people do not think of Excel as XML. The same goes for XBRL.

XML describes semi-structured documents that look like trees. XBRL describes facts organized in a tabular and structured way. For the record, XBRL does support hierarchies for organizing the metadata, but these hierarchies are not expressed using natural XML hierarchies: they are expressed using linkbases (XLink) as flat lists of edges.

So, XBRL is not XML and one could imagine having alternate syntaxes such as JSON or YAML or, for all we know, Markdown.

1.4.2   XBRL is complicated

Certainly, if you open an XBRL instance and taxonomy in a text editor and view the XML syntax, you will find it to be very complicated. If you attempt to read the original specifications, you will find very precise and intricate technical language.

Yet, the burden of this complexity should be, and is increasingly carried by the designers of XBRL tools. Only they programmatically manipulate XBRL at the XML level, and only they (should) read the specifications to ensure they are compliant.

From a user's perspective, XBRL is not very complicated to understand, and the best XBRL tools are the ones that manage to shield their users from the machinery. In the end, creating or reading XBRL filings should not be more complicated than using spreadsheet software.

1.4.3   XBRL is only for business reporting

Business reporting: this is what the B and the R in XBRL stand for. Yet XBRL is much more general that this and pretty much anything can be stored in the XBRL format.

1.4.4 XBRL does not scale up

Most vendors are able to validate XBRL data at the level of a filing. It is a challenge to make XBRL scale up in the sense that you can process the data over hundreds, thousands of filings. But not impossible. Actually, because XBRL cuts data into small atoms — facts — that all look alike from far away, it is all set for scaling up elegantly.

1.4.5 XBRL lacks of standardization

XBRL *is* a standard. It standardizes business reporting like it has never been done before. This is even the primary reason why the use of XBRL should be encouraged.

Of course, it still gives a lot of freedom to users: there are lots of different ways to express the same data in XBRL. There can still be some heterogeneity in the way companies build their metadata hierarchies, or in the terminology they use. Yet also this can be standardized, XBRL lays the groundwork for further standardization on a higher level. This is no different from languages such as C++ being very powerful, and companies enforcing styleguides to restrict their usage to a simpler subset.

In XBRL, some styleguides, also called application profiles, are already establishing themselves, for example many reporting authorities are taking over most SEC practices, and another practice establishing itself, for example in EBA filings (COREP, FINREP), is called the DPM (Data Point Model). The DPM is to XBRL a bit what REST is to HTTP: REST is "HTTP done right," and one could say the DPM — or at least, its core idea because its design goes beyond this — is "XBRL done right," in that it re-expresses the semantics of identifying and slicing and dicing facts in XBRL in a clean way. To be fair to other practices, all of them do in fact adhere to the DPM's core principles.

1.5   Samples

Some samples of XBRL instances, taxonomy schemata and linkbases are available online at `http://ghislainfourny.github.io/the-xbrl-book/samples.html`. More will be added.

These samples are provided as a complement to the material covered in this book. They can be opened in a text or XML editor for those who are interested in understanding the XML syntax, but they can also be opened by XBRL processors to be viewed on a higher level and without worrying about syntax.

They are grouped by chapter, and were designed in such a way that they only use the material covered so far.

1.6   What is new in the second edition

The main contribution of the second edition is the new chapter on hypercubes, which introduces hypercube, dimension, member and line-items report elements, as well as hypercube validation and definition linkbases. We also added more information on the differences between presentation-based reports and DPM-based reports.

1.7   Pedagogical approach of this book

The philosophy of the book stays identical to the first edition and revolves about Edgar Codd's data independence.

1.7.1   Learning XBRL independently from XML

In each chapter, we introduce the XBRL data model independently of XML, and the XML syntax is only introduced in the last section, leveraging all the knowledge previously acquired.

1.7.2 Step by step

Each chapter builds on the previous ones, i.e., we took particular care in only using conceptual building blocks after having introduced them.

1.7.3 Pedagogical terminology

Unlike a specification, a book is intended to be read by end users and thus is formulated and structured in a different way. For pedagogical purposes, the terminology used here can thus slightly deviate from the wording in the specifications. Our terminology (the six kinds of report elements, granularity of a network, etc), is largely inspired by Charles Hoffman's work and, most importantly, allows explaining the XBRL data model all by itself. However, we do our best to give the equivalent terminology used in specifications in footnotes whenever we can. We hope that the reader will realize that, once the overall data model of XBRL is understood, terminology is really only terminology.

1.7.4 Two main paradigms

Two main paradigms for XBRL reporting cohabit in the industry: presentation-based and DPM-based. As the latter is more difficult to master, we believe in the pedagogical value of first learning how to build and understand presentation-based reports. Learning the DPM approach is then much easier. This is why this book largely focuses on presentation-based, EDGAR-style reports, while referring when appropriate to the specificities of the DPM approach. A subsequent edition of the book will also cover table linkbases, on which DPM reports rely.

1.8   Acknowledgments

Credits are to be given to Charles Hoffman, as the samples and
some examples in this book are largely derived and adapted from
the samples that he designed to support and showcase his work on
commonly used patterns. He made amazing contributions to the
XBRL community with his insights.

Some other real-life examples are taken from publicly available
reports such as those submitted to the SEC. Others are simply
made up.

My sincere thanks also go to all the people who supported me
throughout the writing of the book with advice, insights and constructive feedback.

It is always possible that I overlooked a few things or that there
are some typos. Constructive feedback is always welcome and will
be considered in subsequent editions or releases.

Chapter 2

Facts

The R in XBRL stands for reporting. If XBRL could be summarized in one single definition, it would be this: XBRL is about reporting facts. In this chapter, we introduce the notion of a fact, analyze in details what it is made of, to finally arrive at the raw syntax in which this fact is reported in an XBRL instance.

2.1 Atoms of data

The XBRL paradigm is based on the idea that data can be broken into very small chunks, in such a way that each chunk makes sense all by itself, while being irreducible to anything smaller, at least in a meaningful way. Hence, each of these chunks can be seen as an atom of data. These chunks are called facts.

An example of fact is that Coca Cola had $91,016,000,000 of assets as of April 3, 2015. Another example of fact is that the π constant is 3.1415 with a precision of 4 decimals, at all times.

A fact is a value that carries a context. In the first example, the value is 91,016,000,000, while the context specifies that these are the assets owned by Coca Cola on April 3, 2015, in U.S. dollars.

The context is crucial: the value alone would be useless, and it is the context that makes the fact self-explaining. If you simply give the value 91,016,000,000, and only this value, to somebody else, this person will not be able to do much, except maybe look for its mathematical properties. If however you give this value together with its context, that is, the entire fact, to another person, they will have all they need to understand it, and reuse it in a different environment, for example to generate a fiscal report for the company at hand, or a comparison across Dow 30 companies. As such, a fact is not only data, it is information.

2.2   Aspects

Let us now look more carefully to contexts. One of the requirements of XBRL is that, even though a fact can be understood by a human, it can also be processed by a machine. This implies that a context cannot be an informal description of what the value is about: it must have some structure.

Indeed, a context is made of a list of characteristics that qualify the fact. In our first example, the context associated with the value 91,016,000,000 has the following characteristics:

- These are assets;

- They belong to Coca Cola;

- The value is true as of April 3, 2015;

- They are expressed in U.S. dollars.

Looking closer, it can be seen that each characteristic is made of what is called an aspect, and of a value associated to this aspect. We can rewrite the above context as follows:

- What: Assets;

- Who: Coca Cola;

- When : April 3, 2015;

- Of what: U.S. dollars.

In this simple example, the aspects used are all standard XBRL aspects, in that they are specifically defined in the XBRL specifications because of their universality: The aspect describing what a value is about is called Concept. The aspect describing about whom this value is is called Entity. The aspect describing when this value holds is called Period, and the aspect describing the unit of the value is called Unit. So, a form of the context that is now very close to the way a fact is reported in XBRL[1] is:

- Concept: Assets;

- Entity: Coca Cola;

- Period: April 3, 2015;

- Unit: U.S. dollars.

Many more aspects can be created and used to describe the context of a fact, for example geographical aspects such as countries, or company subdivisions, what-if scenarios, the time at which the fact was reported or updated, and so forth.

---

[1] At that point, the reader familiar with the XBRL specification may point out that XBRL excludes concepts and units, as well as languages, from the context associated with a fact. However, this is more a technical detail than something that is semantically relevant to XBRL, and concepts as well as units are still considered aspects in other XBRL specifications. For pedagogical purposes, it is much easier to consider that they are part of the context as well, which we do here. Also from a data model perspective, this is the right thing to do.

Aspect	Characteristic
Concept	Assets
Entity	Coca Cola
Period	April 3, 2015
Unit	U.S. Dollars
Fact value	91,016,000,000

Figure 2.1: Our example fact in tabular form, one characteristic per row.

2.3 The tabular model

With this last description of the context, it should by now have become apparent that XBRL, and facts in general, are of a tabular nature. A single fact can be displayed as shown on Figure 2.1.

Because of this structure, several facts can be displayed in a table form: this is called a fact table. In a fact table, each fact appears in a row, and each column corresponds to an aspect, plus one column for the value. For example, one can include further facts from the same fiscal report, as shown on Figure 2.2.

Figure 2.3 shows another fact table that contains textual facts. It does not have any Unit aspect, but a Language aspect is present. Figure 2.4 shows a fact table merging the first two. It has empty cells because not all aspects apply for all facts.

2.4 Instances

When facts are reported, they are batched and reported in what is called an XBRL instance. Often, it can also be called a report or a filing. An XBRL instance can simply be seen as a flat list of facts. For example, the quarterly report of Coca Cola submitted to the SEC for the fiscal period Q1 2015 is an XBRL instance.

Concept	Entity	Period	Unit	Value
Assets	Coca Cola	April 3, 2015	U.S. Dollars	91,016,000,000
Assets	Coca Cola	December 31, 2014	U.S. Dollars	92,023,000,000
Assets, Current	Coca Cola	April 3, 2015	U.S. Dollars	32,119,000,000
Assets, Current	Coca Cola	December 31, 2014	U.S. Dollars	32,986,000,000
Other Assets, Noncurrent	Coca Cola	April 3, 2015	U.S. Dollars	4,602,000,000
Other Assets, Noncurrent	Coca Cola	December 31, 2014	U.S. Dollars	4,407,000,000

Figure 2.2: A fact table, displaying several monetary facts in structured form, one fact per row.

Concept	Entity	Period	Language	Value
Name	USA	January 1, 2016	English	United States of America
Name	USA	January 1, 2016	German	États-Unis d'Amérique
Name	USA	January 1, 2016	French	Vereinigte Staaten von Amerika

Figure 2.3: A fact table, displaying several textual facts in structured form, one fact per row.

Taking the example of the yearly and quarterly fiscal reports submitted to the SEC, an XBRL instance typically reports between 500 and 2000 facts.

2.5 Collisions

So, an XBRL instance can be seen as a bag of facts, with each fact having a value and a context against which this value makes sense. A question that arises naturally is: what happens if several facts are reported against the same context, in other words, if facts collide with each other? Can it happen at all?

The answer to the latter question is yes. Not only can it happen, because the XBRL specification does not specifically forbid it, but it also does happen in practice. There are several approaches to the question of colliding facts.

2.5.1 Why it is a good thing to allow them

Intuitively, it would seem like a good idea to simply forbid fact collisions. But it would be unfeasible in practice. At the scale of a single XBRL instance of course, it is an easy task to check for collisions, because there are not so many facts. Actually, good XBRL software should probably warn you if you are attempting to generate an instance with colliding facts.

However, on much bigger scales, such as all instances submitted to an authority, or even all XBRL instances worldwide, this is

Concept	Entity	Period	Unit	Language	Value
Assets	Coca Cola	April 3, 2015	U.S. Dollars		91,016,000,000
Assets	Coca Cola	December 31, 2014	U.S. Dollars		92,023,000,000
Assets, Current	Coca Cola	April 3, 2015	U.S. Dollars		32,119,000,000
Assets, Current	Coca Cola	December 31, 2014	U.S. Dollars		32,986,000,000
Other Assets, Noncurrent	Coca Cola	April 3, 2015	U.S. Dollars		4,602,000,000
Other Assets, Noncurrent	Coca Cola	December 31, 2014	U.S. Dollars		4,407,000,000
Name	USA	January 1, 2016		English	United States of America
Name	USA	January 1, 2016		German	États-Unis d'Amérique
Name	USA	January 1, 2016		French	Vereinigte Staaten von Amerika

Figure 2.4: A fact table, displaying several textual and monetary facts in structured form, one fact per row.

simply unrealistic, because we are talking billions and billions of facts, distributed across millions of machines. Of course, it could happen some day, if XBRL becomes mainstream and establishes itself, that some standardized mechanism and infrastructure allows for a worldwide collision detection, but there is nothing like this yet as of 2015.

Furthermore, it is not necessarily a bad thing to allow for collisions to happen. The recent experience in the database world showed that one can handle much vaster quantities of data if one gives up, or at least makes compromises on, consistency. Concretely, if collisions are allowed, it makes it much simpler and more efficient to scale up the production, exchange and storage of XBRL facts.

2.5.2   Detect a collision

Collisions can be detected by comparing contexts: if two facts have the exact same aspects, and each one of these aspects is associated with the same value for both facts, then these facts are duplicates and collide. The XBRL specification provides more involved technical machinery to describe this[2], but this is the essence of it.

2.5.3   Amendments

What to do when a collision is detected depends on the values of the colliding facts: if these values are identical, the facts are consistent with each other. If however the values diverge, it requires more care in the semantics of this divergence.

A very common use case found in practice is that of amendments. In the United States, companies that report to the SEC have the possibility to resubmit facts with updated values, either

---

[2]Equality predicates such as structure equality, value equality, parent equality, context equality, unit equality and XPath equality, defined recursively

in a special amended report, or in the next period. For example, a fact reported in a Q1 report (a 10-Q report) may be updated in the next Q2 report (also 10-Q), or in a Q1 amendment report (a 10-Q/A report).

In this case, the collision is easy to solve: the latest reported value has to be taken. A more involved solution would involve adding an aspect with the time at which the fact was reported (database people call this "transaction time", which removes the collision completely).

2.6 Precision and decimals

In an ideal world, for example in mathematics, values are exact. Any physicist will however tell you that, in practice, values are always given with a margin of error, or at a certain precision.

XBRL supports annotating a fact value with information about its precision.

For example, let us consider the following value, $\frac{22}{7}$, which is an approximation of π:

$$3.142857$$

The first few digits are correct, however at some point, it deviates from the actual value of π. Let us distinguish the digits that are accurate from those that aren't with a vertical bar.

$$3.14|2857$$

XBRL provides two different frameworks for expressing exactly this:

- *Precision of 3*: The first 3 significant digits (that is, not including any zeros in the front: 3, 1 and 4) are correct;

- *2 Decimals*: The value is correct up to 2 digits after the decimal period (1 and 4).

Let us take another example: the Earth-Sun distance (astronomical unit), of which we consider that the trailing zeros are imprecise:

$$149,597,870,7|00$$

This leads to a negative value of the Decimals property, because this time the imprecision happens before the period:

- *Precision of 10*: The first 10 significant digits (1, 4, 9, 5, 9, 7, 8, 7, 0, 7) are correct;

- *-2 Decimals*: The value is correct up to 2 digits *before* the decimal period.

The two ways are equivalent, in that, given the precision, it is possible to infer the decimals, and given the decimals, it is possible to infer the precision.

For example, let us go back to the assets of Coca Cola on April 3, 2015. Typically, values in balance sheets are given up -3 or -6 decimals after the period (the last 3 or 6 digits before the period are not considered precise). In the present case, Coca Cola reported them with -6 decimals:

$$91,016|,000,000$$

Since this number has 11 digits before the period, we can equivalently say that the value has a precision of $11 + (-6)$, that is, 5 significant digits.

There is a special value for infinity, used for exact representations: if the value reported is exact, it has infinite Precision and an infinite number of Decimals.

When an XBRL instance is produced, exactly one of the two properties, precision or decimals, has to be provided. The other property also exists in any case, but it will be inferred automatically.

2.7 Basic aspects

Facts have a context made of characteristics, and each characteristic is a value associated to an aspect. The number of aspects in facts is virtually only limited by imagination. However, there are a few ones that are standard and common and that we describe here: concept, entity, period and unit. All facts have a concept, entity and period, but not necessarily a unit.

Further chapters will introduce how new aspects (called *dimensions*) can be created and used.

For ease of language and for the sake of a smoother read, we will use the terminology "concept of a fact" to mean "the value associated with the concept aspect in the context of the fact", and likewise for the other aspects ("period of a fact", "entity of a fact", "unit of a fact").

2.7.1 Concept

The concept aspect describes *what* the value is. For example, it can be assets, or it can be income, or it can be the total of a bill.

Concepts are the most important aspect in XBRL, and are described in greater detail in Chapter 3. In particular, the concept of a fact has an implication on what value, period and unit is allowed.

Internally, they are identified with qualified names, which are described in Section 3.3.

2.7.2   Entity

The entity aspect describes about *whom* the fact is. In the very widespread case of fiscal reports, it is the company that is reporting their own fundamentals.

Entities are identified in a way that can change from country to country, from stock exchange to stock exchange, or even from regulator to regulator. In the USA, the SEC assigns so-called CIKs (Central Index Keys) to all companies, for example Coca Cola has CIK 21344. XBRL allows for any scheme, but of course requires that you specify which scheme you use every time an entity is identified.

2.7.3   Period

The period aspect describes *when* the fact is valid (database experts will know this as *valid time*, as opposed to *transaction time*).

XBRL allows for two kinds of periods:

- Instant periods, which can be a single point in time, such as April 3, 2015 or November 11, 2011 at 11:11am.

- Duration periods, such as January 1st, 2014 thru June 30th, 2014. A special kind of duration period is the forever period, which means that the fact is valid at all times.

Whenever a time is not specified but only a date is given, the time is implicitly assumed to be midnight at the end of the day, that is, $24:00^3$.

---

[3]Which is equivalent to midnight at the beginning of the following day, the latter being used in the specification for technical reasons.

2.7.4 Unit

The unit aspect describes what the value designates, in other terms, whether what is being counted is apples or pears.

Units can be simple, such as currencies (U.S. Dollar, Swiss Franc, Euro, British Pound, Japanese Yen and so on) but also as complex as physical units with products and possibly a ratio: m, km/h, $N.m^2/kg^2$ or also, say, for dividends, dollars per shares, and so on.

XBRL defines standard units such as *pure* and *share*, and many more in unit registries.

There are some constraints on the usage of units. For example, if the fact value is not a number, the fact cannot have a unit aspect at all (not even the pure unit). Or if the fact value is expressed in a currency, then the unit must be a currency code following the ISO 4217 standard.

Units will be described in more details in Section 3.4. Internally, they are identified with qualified names, which are described in Section 3.3.

2.7.5 Language

The language aspect describes in what language the value of the fact is (English, German, Japanese...), in case it is textual. The value of this aspect must be a language code, as described in Section 4.3.

This aspect can only appear on facts that report a string value.

Note that the XBRL specifications diverge regarding whether the language of a fact value should be an aspect or not. The core XBRL specification will consider facts in multiple language as duplicates, hence not considering language an aspect. The same goes in an official document about duplicates in XBRL, which leaves it to the filers to have or not facts in multiple languages.

However, the newer Open Information Model working draft considers languages an aspect, and we think that this is the right way to go from a data modeling perspective.

2.8 XML syntax of an XBRL instance

Hopefully, upon reading this chapter, the reader should have forgotten that XBRL is XML, and if so, then it means that the author's point came across that XBRL really *is not* XML, even if it *uses* the XML syntax, and could use any other semi-structured syntax such as JSON or YAML.

Since XML is the standard syntax used to store and transfer XBRL facts, though, this book would not be complete if it did not also give a few hints on how this syntax looks like. In this section, we describe how XBRL facts are encoded in XML.

The first important point is that, in the XML syntax, a fact, that is, its value and its context, is split into three parts:

- The context, but without the concept and the unit;

- The unit;

- The concept and the value of the fact.

In the raw XBRL specification, contexts exclude concepts and units. To avoid any ambiguity, we will continue to use the word context including them, but refer to contexts that exclude them as *syntactic contexts*, or use a teletype font such as `xbrli:context`.

The main motivation is re-usability: syntactic contexts and units can be shared and reused across several facts, which saves a lot of space.

2.8.1 XML content ahead

The readers who do not intend to use or look at the XML syntax of XBRL can safely skip the remainder of this section, as well as all sections on the XML syntax of XBRL in each chapter. This is typically the case for users and consumers of an XBRL processor, who have the ability and luxury to work on a more abstract level than the syntax.

From the sake of simplicity and modularity, we assume from now on that the reader is already familiar with the XML and XML Schema technologies. In particular for this section, we assume that the reader knows about XML concepts such as elements, attributes, text, comments, QNames and namespaces. If such is not the case, we kindly refer to books on the matter, as knowing XML and XML Schema well is strongly advisable for any engineer who needs to directly produce, read or update XBRL syntax. This is typically the case for developers of XBRL processors.

We will introduce the XML syntax of XBRL through examples rather than schemata or detailed descriptions, in order to convey the overall taste of it. For reference or specific clarifications, the XBRL specification remains the ideal place to look up.

2.8.2 Overall structure

So, how does an XBRL instance look like (at least the part that contains the facts)? It is made of a root `xbrli:xbrl` element, of which the children are `xbrli:context`, `xbrli:unit` and fact elements (the actual facts), which reference contexts and units.

Namespaces

The `xbrli:xbrl`, `xbrli:context`, `xbrli:unit` elements are all in the XBRL instance namespace `http://www.xbrl.org/2003/instance`, which is typically associated with the prefix `xbrli`. Often, it

```
<?xml version="1.0"?>
<xbrli:xbrl xmlns:xbrli="http://www.xbrl.org/2003/instance">
  <xbrli:context>
    <!-- context definition -->
  </xbrli:context>
  <!-- more contexts -->

  <xbrli:unit>
    <!-- unit definition -->
  </xbrli:unit>
  <!-- more units -->

  <!-- facts -->
</xbrli:xbrl>
```

(use contexts)

(use units)

Figure 2.5: The skeleton of an XBRL instance: first contexts, then units, then facts. Each fact references a context and a unit.

is made the default namespace for less verbosity, but for pedagogical reasons, we will use the prefix xbrli throughout this book.

So, the skeleton of an XBRL instance, would be as shown on Figure 2.5, with at least one context and one fact mandatory.

We will now go into more details about each of the three kinds of elements.

2.8.3   Context

The syntactic xbrli:context describes the context of the fact, that is, all aspects except concept, unit and language. Since for now, we have only seen entity and period, we will only give the syntax for these two and come back to it later with new aspects.

Figure 2.6 shows a context element that contains an entity and a period definition. A context must be identified with an id attribute, so that facts can refer to it. The semantics of id attributes

```
<xbrli:context
    xmlns:xbrli="http://www.xbrl.org/2003/instance"
    id="cocacola-in-april">

  <xbrli:entity>
    <xbrli:identifier scheme="http://www.sec.gov/CIK">
      0000021344 <!-- This would be Coca Cola -->
    </xbrli:identifier>
  </xbrli:entity>

  <xbrli:period>
    <xbrli:instant>2015-04-03</xbrli:instant>
  </xbrli:period>

</xbrli:context>
```

Figure 2.6: An `xbrli:context` element. It contains at least the entity and period – but not the concept and unit.

is that defined by XML, in particular they must be unique within an XML document.

Entity

In a context, the entity is defined with an `xbrli:entity` element that has an `xbrli:identifier` child element.

The `xbrli:identifier` element is made of a **scheme** attribute URI and a value. The value is simply a string, and its format depends on the scheme used. In the example on Figure 2.6, the scheme used is the official CIK scheme of the Securities and Exchange Commission. The CIK of Coca Cola is 21344, but they are typically extended to a 10-digit string.

Period

The period is defined with a `xbrli:period` element. Its children depend on the kind of period. Figure 2.7 shows further examples of syntax for periods.

An instant period uses a single `xbrli:instant` element. The `xbrli:instant` has an XML Schema type of either `xs:date` or `xs:dateTime`, that is, a union of these types. Both formats use ISO 8601, with lexical values such as "2015-10-30" for an `xs:date` or "2015-10-30T08:00:00.000Z" for an `xs:dateTime`.

A duration period, which is a time interval, needs to specify two points in time instead of just one: a starting point and an ending point. Hence, it has two child elements: `xbrli:startDate` and `xbrli:endDate`. Both `xbrli:startDate` and `xbrli:endDate` are of type either `xs:date` or `xs:dateTime`, in the same way as instant periods.

An exception is the special duration period "forever", which is represented with simply an empty `xbrli:forever` element.

The elements `xbrli:instant`, `xbrli:startDate` and `xbrli:endDate` call all contain a value of the XML Schema Types date or dateTime.

```
<xbrli:period
    xmlns:xbrli="http://www.xbrl.org/2003/instance">
  <xbrli:instant>2015-04-03T12:00:00</xbrli:instant>
</xbrli:period>
```

(a) An instant period, in this case an `xs:dateTime`

```
<xbrli:period
    xmlns:xbrli="http://www.xbrl.org/2003/instance">
  <xbrli:startDate>2015-04-03</xbrli:startDate>
  <xbrli:endDate>2015-10-03</xbrli:endDate>
</xbrli:period>
```

(b) A duration period (except forever), in this case `xs:dates`

```
<xbrli:period
    xmlns:xbrli="http://www.xbrl.org/2003/instance">
  <xbrli:forever/>
</xbrli:period>
```

(c) A forever period

Figure 2.7: The XML syntax for each kind of period – forever, even though it is a duration, has a different syntax.

2.8.4   Unit

Units are defined in a way similar to contexts, using the `xbrli:unit` element, and also require an `id` attribute so facts can refer to them. The most basic units are straightforward to define with a `xbrli:measure` child element. Unit values are QNames, so you need to bind any namespace you may need, such as the standard ISO 4217 namespace for all currencies. More details on standardized units are given in Section 3.4.

Figure 2.8 shows a few examples of unit elements.

You can build product units, like square feet or kWh, by appending more `xbrli:measure` elements.

Ratio units are slightly more complex, and require inserting a `xbrli:divide` element with two children, `xbrli:unitNumerator` and, as you may already have guessed, `xbrli:unitDenominator`. The `xbrli:measure` element can then be used in each of these two grandchildren elements.

```
<xbrli:unit
    xmlns:xbrli="http://www.xbrl.org/2003/instance"
    xmlns:ISO4217="http://www.xbrl.org/2003/iso4217"
    id="dollars">
  <xbrli:measure>ISO4217:USD</xbrli:measure>
</xbrli:unit>
```

(a) A dollar unit

```
<xbrli:unit
    xmlns:xbrli="http://www.xbrl.org/2003/instance"
    id="pure">
  <xbrli:measure>xbrli:pure</xbrli:measure>
</xbrli:unit>
```

(b) A pure (dimensionless) unit

```
<xbrli:unit
    xmlns:xbrli="http://www.xbrl.org/2003/instance"
    xmlns:ISO4217="http://www.xbrl.org/2003/iso4217"
    id="francs-per-share">
  <xbrli:divide>

    <xbrli:unitNumerator>
      <xbrli:measure>ISO4217:CHF</xbrli:measure>
    </xbrli:unitNumerator>

    <xbrli:unitDenominator>
      <xbrli:measure>xbrli:shares</xbrli:measure>
    </xbrli:unitDenominator>

  </xbrli:divide>
</xbrli:unit>
```

(c) A more complex unit, with a numerator and a denominator

Figure 2.8: Three examples of unit elements: an ISO 4217 currency, a standard unit, and a unit with a division.

2.8.5 Concept and value

Now that the machinery for defining syntactic contexts and units has been introduced, we can move to the most important piece: elements that define facts.

Unlike `xbrli:context` and `xbrli:unit` elements, facts are defined with a dynamic element name, and this name is that of the concept. You guessed correctly: this implies that concepts are actually syntactically QNames. We will see in later chapters that they can be associated with labels to be displayed so as not to confuse the end users.

Figure 2.9 shows the syntax that describes our running example in this chapter: the assets Coca Cola reported for April 3, 2015, in U.S. dollars. As we will see in Chapter 3, concept names are defined and grouped in namespaces. The concepts used with the SEC are part of the US GAAP (Generally Accepted Accounting Principles) taxonomy, and live in the corresponding namespace[4].

For each fact, two attributes are used to reference the context and unit: `contextRef` and `unitRef`. Either the precision or the decimals can be reported – but not both – with respectively the `precision` and `decimals` attributes. The `precision` attribute has to be a positive integer, and the `decimals` attribute has to be an integer. However, both can also have the special value "INF" for infinite precision.

Finally, the language aspect, if any, is syntactically represented with an `xml:lang` attribute according to the XML specification. Figure 2.10 shows how this is done. Note that, since languages only apply to string values, `xml:lang` will never appear with `unitRef`, `decimals` or `precision`. The `xml` prefix does not need to be bound to the XML namespace, because it is builtin in XML. Figure 2.10

---

[4]The namespace is actually updated every year to a new version. It makes comparisons across years more complicated, but still doable. More on this in Section 3.3.

```
<us-gaap:Assets
    xmlns:us-gaap="http://fasb.org/us-gaap/2015-01-31"
    contextRef="cocacola-in-april"
    unitRef="dollars"
    decimals="-6">
  91016000000
</us-gaap:Assets>
```

Figure 2.9: The syntax of our first fact example

```
<countries:Name
    xmlns:countries="http://www.example.com/countries"
    contextRef="context1"
    xml:lang="en-US">
  United States of America
</countries:Name>
<countries:Name
    xmlns:countries="http://www.example.com/countries"
    contextRef="context1"
    xml:lang="de">
  Vereinigte Staaten von Amerika
</countries:Name>
<countries:Name
    xmlns:countries="http://www.example.com/countries"
    contextRef="context1"
    xml:lang="fr">
  Etats-Unis d'Amerique
</countries:Name>
```

Figure 2.10: Reporting equivalent facts in three different languages using a hypothetical country name concept. This assumes the existence of a syntactic context called context1 referencing the USA as an entity.

shows the syntax of the three facts formerly introduced in Figure 2.3.

Let us now wrap up. Figure 2.11 brings all three syntactic components together and shows the final XBRL instance reporting our example fact.

```
<?xml version="1.0"?>
<xbrli:xbrl
    xmlns:xbrli="http://www.xbrl.org/2003/instance"
    xmlns:us-gaap="http://fasb.org/us-gaap/2015-01-31"
    xmlns:ISO4217="http://www.xbrl.org/2003/iso4217">

  <xbrli:context id="cocacola-in-april">
    <xbrli:entity>
      <xbrli:identifier scheme="http://www.sec.gov/CIK">
        0000021344 <!-- This would be Coca Cola -->
      </xbrli:identifier>
    </xbrli:entity>
    <xbrli:period>
      <xbrli:instant>2015-04-03</xbrli:instant>
    </xbrli:period>
  </xbrli:context>
                                                  (reference)
  <xbrli:unit id="dollars">
    <xbrli:measure>
      ISO4217:USD
    </xbrli:measure>
  </xbrli:unit>
                               (reference)
  <us-gaap:Assets
      contextRef="cocacola-in-april"
      unitRef="dollars"
      decimals="-6">
    91016000000
  </us-gaap:Assets>

</xbrli:xbrl>
```

Figure 2.11: A complete XBRL instance, with a `xbrli:context`, `xbrli:unit` as well as fact element named after its concept. Typically, an instance has a lot of contexts, units and facts, often on the order of magnitude of hundreds or thousands. Facts can share the contexts and units they reference, to save space.

2.8.6   Validation and correctness

We have just introduced the heart of XBRL: facts, and their XML
syntax. We saw how to express a fact in XML, and how to define the contexts and units that they are associated with. This is
an important basis for understanding XBRL. After finishing this
chapter, you should be able to produce your own XBRL instances,
but also to read and understand existing ones.

   The document shown on Figure 2.11 is actually not quite complete: it is an XML document, it is well-formed, but it is not
valid, because we have not introduced any schema yet to validate
it against.

   In fact, XBRL leverages XML Schema to validate XBRL instances. In XBRL, an XML Schema is called a taxonomy schema.
An instance can point to one or several taxonomy schemata, so
that it can be validated against them.

   The taxonomy schemata can be defined by various institutions,
reporting authorities, companies and people, in order to define the
concepts that they use or that are to be used.

2.8.7   A complete example

A complete instance in the XML syntax can be downloaded online
from the location provided in Section 1.5. This instance can be
found under the samples for Chapter 2. The corresponding fact
table is shown on Figure 2.12.

   The instance contains only material covered in this chapter, so
that everything in it should be understandable to the reader who
has read the entire chapter.

2.9   JSON syntax of an XBRL instance

The Open Information Model defines an alternate JSON syntax for
XBRL instances. It is currently a draft. We will describe it here

oim:concept	oim:entity	oim:period	oim:unit	value
pattern:BasisOfPresentation	samp:SAMP	2010-01-01/2010-12-31		Praesent fringilla feugiat magna. Suspendisse et lorem eu risus convallis placerat.Suspendisse potenti. Donec malesuada loremid mi. Nunc ut purus ac nisl tempus accumsan.
pattern:InventoryValuationMethod	samp:SAMP	2010-01-01/2010-12-31		Cost.
pattern:DescriptionOfInventoryComponents	samp:SAMP	2010-01-01/2010-12-31		Proin elit sem, ornare non, ullamcorper vel, sollicitudin a, lacus. Mauris tincidunt cursus est. Nulla sit amet nibh. Sed elementum feugiat augue. Nam non tortor non leo porta bibendum. Morbi eu pede.
pattern:InventoryCostMethod	samp:SAMP	2010-01-01/2010-12-31		FIFO
pattern:TradeReceivablesPolicy	samp:SAMP	2010-01-01/2010-12-31		Sed magna felis, accumsan a, fermentum quis, varius sed, ipsum. Nullam leo. Donec eros.
pattern:InvestmentsInSecuritiesPolicy	samp:SAMP	2010-01-01/2010-12-31		Etiam ipsum orci, gravida nec, feugiat ut, malesuada quis, mauris. Etiam porttitor. Ut venenatis, velit a accumsan interdum, odio metus mollis mauris, non pharetra augue arcu eu felis.
pattern:BankBorrowingsPolicy	samp:SAMP	2010-01-01/2010-12-31		Ut ut risus nec nibh dictum posuere. Phasellus eleifend, diam vitae dapibus pulvinar, erat ligula auctor dui, eget conguejusto lorem hendrerit tellus.
pattern:ProvisionsPolicySuspendisse	samp:SAMP	2010-01-01/2010-12-31		vestibulum augue eu justo. Pellentesque habitant morbi tristique senectus et netus et malesuada fames ac turpis egestas.
pattern:Land	samp:SAMP	2010-12-31	iso4217:USD	5347000
pattern:Land	samp:SAMP	2009-12-31	iso4217:USD	1147000
pattern:BuildingsNet	samp:SAMP	2010-12-31	iso4217:USD	244508000
pattern:BuildingsNet	samp:SAMP	2009-12-31	iso4217:USD	366375000
pattern:FurnitureAndFixturesNet	samp:SAMP	2010-12-31	iso4217:USD	34457000
pattern:FurnitureAndFixturesNet	samp:SAMP	2009-12-31	iso4217:USD	34457000
pattern:ComputerEquipmentNet	samp:SAMP	2010-12-31	iso4217:USD	4166000
pattern:ComputerEquipmentNet	samp:SAMP	2009-12-31	iso4217:USD	5313000
pattern:OtherPropertyPlantAndEquipmentNet.	samp:SAMP	2010-12-31	iso4217:USD	6702000
pattern:OtherPropertyPlantAndEquipmentNet.	samp:SAMP	2009-12-31	iso4217:USD	6149000
pattern:PropertyPlantAndEquipmentNet.	samp:SAMP	2010-12-31	iso4217:USD	295183000
pattern:PropertyPlantAndEquipmentNet.	samp:SAMP	2009-12-31	iso4217:USD	413441000

Figure 2.12: The fact table (logical view) of the instance chapter-2-instance.xml

when it reaches a mature status.

2.10   Facts and taxonomies

With only facts, XBRL would not go very far: if everybody picked
their own concept names and conventions, the benefit of automation would be completely lost, as no comparison is even possible.
In the next chapter, you will discover how dictionaries of concepts
– taxonomy schemata – can be defined, and how, for each concept,
the allowed fact values as well as the units are restricted. That
way, people can agree on naming their concepts and share their
data consistently.

Chapter 3

Concepts

We can communicate with each other because we use languages and agree on the meaning of the words we use. If everybody spoke their own, random language, there would be no way to understand each other.

XBRL is no different. If everybody reported their facts picking and inventing their own concepts, the reports created this way would not be inter-operable at all. There would be no way to compare facts with each other, nor to do any meaningful analysis on a big fact corpus.

3.1 The nature of facts

We saw in Chapter 2 that concepts are one of the four basis aspects that make up the context against which facts are built.

The concept aspect has something particular about it: it is the only indispensable aspect. While it is true that XBRL does require an entity, a period and when applicable a unit, one can still think of circumventing this obligation by using a special entity that represents the whole world, a forever period, and a pure (i.e., non physically dimensional, see Section 2.8.4) unit. But imagining a special concept that would represent everything is close to impossible[1]. and would have no semantic meaning: you can only report a value by stating what it describes.

3.2 Taxonomies

In order to report facts in a manner consistent with each other, XBRL users agree with each other on the concepts they use by means of a taxonomy. In practice, a taxonomy is built by a reporting authority such as the SEC in the United States, and companies are required to use them. Nevertheless, XBRL is flexible enough to allow for taxonomies to be reused, modified and extended at will.

A taxonomy is made of:

- taxonomy schemata, which are concept definitions;

- and of taxonomy linkbases, which organize concepts in graphs.

In this chapter, we introduce taxonomy schemata. Taxonomy linkbases will be introduced the latter in Chapter 4.

3.2.1 Taxonomy schemata

A taxonomy schema, to put it in simple words, is a dictionary of concept names, together with some more meta-information as well as constraints about the facts that use them, such as a restriction on the type of the fact value, or the type of period. It can be seen as flat list of concepts.

3.2.2 Concept metadata

Each concept in such a taxonomy schema is defined with:

---

[1] String-theory physicists are working on this though

- An internal name that specifies how that concept is canonically identified everywhere else in XBRL (see Section 3.3)

- A data type that specifies which values are allowed in facts that are reported against this concept (see Section 3.4)

- A period type that specifies which kinds of periods are allowed in facts that are reported against this concept (see Section 3.5)

- A balance – for concepts that have a currency data type – mostly useful to accountants (see Section 3.6)

3.2.3 Validation of an instance against a taxonomy schema

A taxonomy schema is a flat list of concepts together with their metadata. An instance is a flat[2] list of facts. Each fact, in its context, uses a concept.

A taxonomy schema (or several of them) can be attached to an instance. Once this is done, it needs to be verified that all facts in the instance use concepts consistently in accordance to their definition in the taxonomy schema, as shown on Figure 3.1.

For example, in the US GAAP taxonomy schema, the `us-gaap:Assets` concept has a data type of `xbrli:monetaryItemType` and an instant period type. This means that, if a fact is reported against the concept `us-gaap:Assets` in an instance, and the period of this fact is a duration, or the value of this fact is a Boolean, then a validation error needs to be reported.

3.2.4 Discoverable Taxonomy Sets

An XBRL instance — the data — is attached to a taxonomy. This taxonomy is usually made of many blocks, that is, taxonomy

---

[2]We are leaving tuples out of the discussion for now

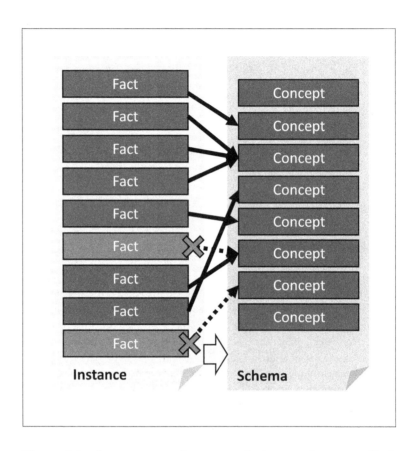

Figure 3.1: A taxonomy schema attached to an instance. Each fact in the instance must be consistent with the concepts it uses according to the schema. In this case, two facts are not valid because they use their concept inconsistently.

schemata and linkbases. These schemata and linkbases can be reused, reassembled together and reattached to other instances at will. The set of all schemata and linkbases attached to an instance is called the discoverable taxonomy set, often abbreviated as DTS. Each instance has its own DTS, but several instances may share parts or all of their DTS.

As far as schemata are concerned, the simplest perspective on a DTS is that its taxonomy schemata can be merged together as a single, flat list of concepts — duplicates are not allowed — and the separation as several taxonomy schemata can be seen as a syntactic detail. That way, Figure 3.1 also applies for the entire DTS.

However, XBRL consumers, IT-savvy or not, are usually aware of the fact that concepts are organized and grouped together meaningfully. For example, consumers of the fiscal reports filed to the SEC know that some concepts — assets, revenues, etc. — are part of the US GAAP taxonomy, while some others — fiscal year focus, fiscal period end date, company name, etc. — are part of the DEI (Document and Entity Information) taxonomy, etc. Taxonomy designers also often reuse and extend existing taxonomy schemata to build on them.

An instance and its taxonomy schemata are organized in a DAG[3] in which instances have links to taxonomy schemata, and taxonomy schemata in turn have links to more taxonomy schemata, as shown on Figure 3.2. Later, we will see that this DAG also contains the taxonomy linkbases, but let us keep them aside for now.

The taxonomy schemata in this DAG form the discoverable taxonomy set. More precisely, the DTS attached to an instance is made of all schemata and linkbases that are in the transitive closure of the instance.

When an XBRL report is opened by a processor, the first action it undertakes is to resolve all links to reconstruct the DTS. Then, it can perform validation and check that (i) the taxonomy schemata

---

[3]directed acyclic graph: a directed graph that has no directed cycles

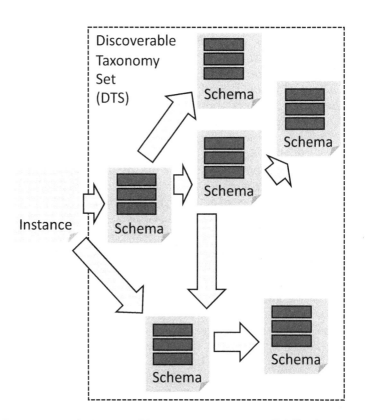

Figure 3.2: A discoverable taxonomy set as a DAG of taxonomy schemata. Taxonomy linkbases are omitted for now.

and linkbases are consistent and (ii) the instance is valid against the DTS.

3.3 Concept names

3.3.1 Qualified names

The concept name that is agreed on to report facts is typically an internal name, very often in English, and this internal name is not intended to be user-friendly. However, end users are able to view concepts in their own language, because their XBRL front-end will display a user-friendly label in any language they want – provided somebody supplied the translation, of course. The label machinery will be described in Chapter 4.

The internal name of the concepts, but also many other internal names in the XBRL world such as units or data types, are so-called *qualified names*, also called SQNames in the new Open Information Model draft. The previous chapter, on purpose, shielded the reader from this machinery. However, it is very useful as an XBRL user to understand how it works.

3.3.2 Namespaces and local names

Qualified names work a bit like first names and family names. Let us take a look, for example, at the concept for describing assets in the US GAAP taxonomy used for fiscal reports. On a fancy display, it will just appear as plain English such as "Assets", or "Total Assets". Internally though, it is made of two bricks:

- a local name (by analogy, a first name): for example Assets. If the local name is made of several words, CamelCase is used as spaces are forbidden. For example, EarningsPerShareTextBlock.

- a namespace URI (Universal Resource Identifier, by analogy, a last name) that often looks just like a URL, even if it is not intended to be used in a browser: for example the namespace used for US GAAP concepts is `http://fasb.org/us-gaap/2014-01-31`. It can also be a URN.

These two bricks together are a qualified name which can be expressed under what is called the Clark notation: `{http://fasb.org/us-gaap/2014-01-31}Assets`. However, you should forget about this notation right now, because the next subsection will introduce the representation of qualified names commonly used in the XBRL community, with prefixes.

In a DTS, concepts are grouped by namespace. In other words, each taxonomy schema within a DTS contains concepts that all share the same namespace. A DTS may contain several taxonomy schemata with identical namespaces, however the local names of the concepts they define must not overlap to avoid any collisions.

In particular, all the concepts defined in the US GAAP taxonomy schema share the same namespace, and have different local names. Another concept in the taxonomy for fiscal reports in another country, such as Japan, may partly use identical local names, but with a different namespace. Namespaces are critical to avoid collisions between several reporting authorities or users defining their own concepts. Anybody can define any concepts they want in their own namespaces, with the convention that they should own the domain name used in the namespace URL, even though there is no technical enforcement of this.

3.3.3   Prefixes (to keep your sanity)

The reader with some degree of familiarity with XBRL may be surprised at this point that we presented qualified names as a pair (local name, namespace URL) like `{http://fasb.org/us-gaap/2014-01-31}Assets` or `{http://fasb.org/us-gaap/2014-01-31}`

`EarningsPerShareTextBlock` because many business users that
are a bit tech-savvy and look at internal names think of these as
"something with a colon in the middle," more like `us-gaap:Assets`
or `us-gaap:EarningsPerShareTextBlock`.

There is a reason for this: this notation with the colon is a
shortcut. In this case, `us-gaap` implicitly refers to the namespace
`http://fasb.org/us-gaap/2014-01-31` to avoid having to refer
to it completely every time, which would be very verbose.

3.3.4 Consistent usage of prefixes

Technically, these shortcuts, called prefixes, are or should be irrelevant to define a concept name, as what really matters is the namespace itself. However, it is common practice in XBRL to stick to the
same prefix for a namespace, at least within the same report (say,
a 10-K). XBRL users then commonly refer to concepts using the
prefix and ignoring the namespace, that is, freezing the namespace-
prefix binding machinery for the entire report. This practice has
recently been formalized under the terminology of SQName in the
first working draft of the Open Information Model.

The namespace-prefix binding is often specified over entire re-
positories: the SEC specifically recommends the usage of certain
bindings (Recommended Namespace Prefix). Even though this is
not a requirement, it is highly recommended to stick to these bindings.

3.3.5 Taxonomy updates

This actually goes further than that: namespaces are often updated
every year when a new taxonomy is created, and the prefix is kept
across years.

For example, the `us-gaap` prefix in US GAAP taxonomy has
been bound recently to the following namespaces in turn:

`http://fasb.org/us-gaap/2012-01-31`

```
http://fasb.org/us-gaap/2013-01-31
http://fasb.org/us-gaap/2014-01-31
http://fasb.org/us-gaap/2015-01-31
```

and most concepts exist throughout these years, such as `us-g` `aap:Assets`. For an XBRL user, this is the one and same concept, and the namespace acts as a taxonomy versioning scheme.

This makes it very convenient to compare facts that were reported in different years if you look at the prefix and ignore the namespace. The readers familiar with XML will probably need to adapt to what is technically an incorrect use of qualified names, but nevertheless is slowly establishing itself in the XBRL community for pragmatic reasons.

From now on, we will progressively be using qualified names to describe concepts, types, units, etc, and we will be heavily using prefixes as proxies to namespaces to follow this established practice. Whenever we do so, the mapping between prefixes and namespaces will be introduced.

3.4   Data types

The most important constraint that accompanies the definition of a concept in a taxonomy is the type of the value that can be associated with it by a fact, in other terms, it defines an acceptable value space for this concept.

XBRL predefines a lot of built-in types that can be used by all taxonomies. These types are as various as strings (text), numbers, dates, amounts of money, Booleans, binary data, and so on. Many of the types are also accompanied by prescriptions on units that make sense for them, for example meters or inches for a value that is a length. The built-in types have been standardized to cover all common use cases in an inter-operable way, and it is not recommended to create new types, unless there is a compelling reason for it.

3.4.1 The data type registry and the units registry

The original XBRL specification introduces a few types, most of them based on XBRL Schema, as well as two standard units (`xb rli:pure` and `xbrli:shares`). Very quickly, it became clear that this was not enough, and that it would make sense to standardize more to avoid ending up with a plethora of redundant type and unit names across XBRL users.

Hence, many data types and units were introduced later in the process of standardizing XBRL. For the sake of flexibility and extensibility, two registries are available online that standardize data types and units that are very commonly used in practice, notably in the US GAAP (The US framework for fiscal reports), IFRS (the international framework for fiscal reports) and EDINET (the Japanese framework for fiscal reports) taxonomies.

The data type registry is available at

`http://www.xbrl.org/dtr/dtr.xml`

while the units registry is available at

`http://www.xbrl.org/utr/utr.xml`

We will do a survey across all these types and units. The above documents are useful for reference and should be straightforward to understand for the reader with technical background. If need be, the XBRL specifications with the same names (data type registry, units registry) will be useful for more details.

3.4.2 Prefix conventions for data types and units

Throughout this section and the book, the prefix bindings shown on Figure 3.3 are used. These are also the prefixes that are commonly used in XBRL reports, and we also recommend to stick to them.

`xbrli` corresponds to all qualified names introduced early in the XBRL specifications. non-numeric and numeric are used for data types introduced later in the data type registry. `utr` and `ISO4217`

Prefix	Namespace
xbrli	`http://www.xbrl.org/2003/instance`
nonnum	`http://www.xbrl.org/dtr/type/non-numeric`
num	`http://www.xbrl.org/dtr/type/numeric`
utr	`http://www.xbrl.org/2009/utr`
ISO4217	`http://www.xbrl.org/2003/iso4217`

Figure 3.3: Namespaces and prefixes commonly used for defining concept types and units.

	Type	Units
Areas	`num:areaItemType`	`utr:acre`, `utr:sqft`, etc.
Volume	`num:volumeItemType`	`utr:ft3`, `utr:l`, `utr:m3`, etc.
Mass	`num:massItemType`	`utr:lb`, `utr:kg`, etc.
Weights	`num:weightItemType`	
Energy	`num:energyItemType`	`utr:J`, `utr:kWh`, etc.
Length	`num:lengthItemType`	`utr:ft`, `utr:m`, `utr:km`, etc.
Memory	`num:memoryItemType`	`utr:B`, `utr:MB`, etc.

Figure 3.4: Physical types, together with a few examples of units. The complete list of units is documented in the units registry.

are used for units introduced later in the units registry, the latter being for currencies designated according to the ISO 4217 standard.

3.4.3 Physical quantities

Quantities that have a physical reality, used among other by physicists, have standardized data types and units.

XBRL standardizes the physical quantities shown in Figure 3.4. For each kind of physical quantity, we specify the qualified name of the type, and the qualified names of some of the allowed units.

Figure 3.5 shows a fact reporting the Earth-Sun distance in km.

Aspect	Aspect value
Concept	`my:distanceToSun`
Entity	The Earth
Period	December 31th, 2015
Unit	`utr:km`
Fact value	150,000,000
Precision	2

Figure 3.5: A fact expressing a length. The concept `my:distance ToSun`, where `my` is bound to some namespace, is assumed to have the data type `num:lengthItemType`. For pedagogical purposes, we use the qualified names of the concept and unit, but an end user would see something more fancy

3.4.4 Amounts of money

Amounts of money can be expressed using one of the monetary item types. The main monetary item type is `xbrli:monetaryItemType`. Further types were later introduced in the data type registry to restrict the value space to either positive amounts, or amounts with no decimals, or both.

These are the qualified names of the four predefined data types used for currencies. The names speak for themselves.

- `xbrli:monetaryItemType`

- `num:noDecimalsMonetaryItemType`

- `num:nonNegativeMonetaryItemType`

- `num:nonNegativeNoDecimalsMonetaryItemType`

A fact reported against a concept that has a monetary data type must use an ISO 4217 unit, that use three-letter local names as specified in the ISO 4217 standard. For example, U.S. dollars

Aspect	Aspect value
Concept	us-gaap:Assets
Entity	AT&T INC.
Period	December 31th, 2014
Unit	ISO4217:USD
Fact value	292,829,000,000
Decimals	-6

Figure 3.6: A monetary fact (the type of the concept `Assets` is `xbrli:monetaryItemType`)

are represented with the qualified name `ISO4217:USD`, while Swiss Francs are represented with `ISO4217:CHF`, Norwegian Krones with `ISO4217:NOK` and Euros with `ISO4217:CHF`.

The allowed values are decimals for all these types, with restrictions that can be inferred from their names. For example, these two:

`num:nonNegativeMonetaryItemType`

`num:nonNegativeNoDecimalsMonetaryItemType`

only accept 0 or positive decimals, and these two:

`num:noDecimalsMonetaryItemType`

`num:nonNegativeNoDecimalsMonetaryItemType`

only have integers in their value spaces.

Figure 3.6 shows a real example of a fact reported against a concept with a monetary type.

3.4.5   Amounts of shares or per share

Amounts of shares can be expressed using the type `xbrli:shares ItemType`, which also restricts the unit to be `xbrli:shares`.

Monetary amounts per share can be expressed using the type `num:perShareItemType`. The associated unit must then be an ISO

Aspect	Aspect value
Concept	us-gaap:CommonStockDividendsPerShareDeclared
Entity	AT&T INC.
Period	April 1st thru June 30, 2015
Unit	iso4217:USD / xbrli:shares
Fact value	.47
Decimals	INF

Figure 3.7: A monetary fact (the type of the concept against which this fact is reported is num:perShareItemType)

4217 unit, divided by the xbrli:shares unit, as shown on Figure 3.7.

The allowed values are all decimals.

3.4.6 Dimensionless numbers, ratios and percentages

There is a special type xbrli:pureItemType for expressing decimals that have no unit — in the field of physics, they are also known as dimensionless — including ratios between two values with the same units, or percentages. For example, an interest rate of 5% (0.05) or a debt-to-equity ratio of 2. It requires the unit to be xbrli:pure, that is, such values are dimensionless.

The allowed values are all decimals, and percentages must be expressed as decimals, that is, 5 % must be expressed as 0.05.

The data type num:percentItemType is also available in order to specify that the value is a percentage (however, it is not to be multiplied by 100, i.e, 5 % must also be expressed as 0.05).

3.4.7   Numeric data types

Most XBRL numeric data types are based on XML Schema. Each
XML Schema type, like `xs:integer`, is redefined in the XBRL
instance namespace (`xbrli`) by adding the ItemType suffix, like `xb
rli:integerItemType`. Furthermore, XBRL introduces a fraction
item type which is a super-set of decimal, i.e., also containing those
fractions that would need an infinite number of decimals in base
10. However, the current working draft of the Open Information
Model discards its usage.

Figure 3.8 is a complete list of the standardized numeric types
in XBRL. There is no restriction on the units that facts can have
when reported against a concept that has one these types. They
can be used together with user-defined units not standardized in
the official XBRL registries.

We refer to the XML Schema standard for all these types except
`xbrli:fractionitemType`.

3.4.8   Non-numeric data types

XBRL facts do not need to all report numeric values. It is also
very common to report chunks of text, or even structured data,
and there is no limit to the size these fact values can have. The
following types can be used to define such concepts.

Below are the non-numeric data types that are standardized in
the data type registry:

- `nonnum:escapedItemType`: supports values that are strings,
  but which were escaped according to the XML standard (using constructs such as & or &x0A;). This type indicates
  to XBRL consuming applications that they should unescape
  these values.

- `nonnum:xmlNodesItemType`: supports values that are escaped
  XML fragments.

Type	Description
xbrli:fractionItemType	any rational number, with an integer numerator and a non-zero integer denominator *(usage not recommended)*
xbrli:decimalItemType	any decimal number (rational numbers that can be written down with digits and a period)
xbrli:floatItemType	a subset of the decimal numbers that can be encoded on 32 bits (familiar to programmers)
xbrli:doubleItemType	a subset of the decimal numbers that can be encoded on 64 bits (familiar to programmers)
xbrli:integerItemType	any integer
xbrli:nonNegativeIntegerItemType	any non-negative integer
xbrli:negativeIntegerItemType	any negative integer
xbrli:nonPositiveIntegerItemType	any non-positive integer
xbrli:positiveIntegerItemType	any positive integer
xbrli:byteItemType	An integer in the interval $[-2^7, 2^7 - 1]$
xbrli:shortItemType	An integer in the interval $[-2^{15}, 2^{15} - 1]$
xbrli:intItemType	An integer in the interval $[-2^{31}, 2^{31} - 1]$
xbrli:longItemType	An integer in the interval $[-2^{63}, 2^{63} - 1]$
xbrli:unsignedByteItemType	An integer the interval in $[0, 2^8 - 1]$
xbrli:unsignedShortItemType	An integer the interval in $[0, 2^{16} - 1]$
xbrli:unsignedIntItemType	An integer the interval in $[0, 2^{32} - 1]$
xbrli:unsignedLongItemType	An integer the interval in $[0, 2^{64} - 1]$

Figure 3.8: A list of the builtin numeric types

- nonnum:xmlItemType: supports values that are escaped XML documents.

- nonnum:textBlockItemType: supports values that are escaped XHTML (potentially mixed with text).

- nonnum:enumerationItemType: supports value spaces that are a finite, enumerable set, of which items are qualified names.

3.4.9   User-defined types

It is also possible to define new types, however XBRL requires that
these types are all restrictions of the above, standardized XBRL
types. It is not allowed to arbitrarily define XML Schema types.

3.5   Period types

A concept must also specify a period type, which can be either a
duration or an instant. Facts reported against a concept must have
a period that is consistent with the period type of the concept.

That is, if the concept has a period type "instant", then the
period of the fact must be an instant period such as January 28th,
2016.

If the concept has a period type "duration", then the period
of the fact must be a duration such as January 1, 2016 through
December 31, 2016. The *forever* period is also considered to be a
duration period that spans the entire timeline.

3.6   Balance

Monetary concepts must also specify a balance , which corresponds
to the common understanding of accountants. A balance can be
either a credit or a debit . Balances will be relevant in Chapter 6
when facts are aggregated with additions and substractions.

3.7   Examples from US-GAAP

Figure 3.9 shows a couple of US GAAP concepts together with their
data type, period type and balance in this order. The ones prefixed
with us-gaap are from the US GAAP taxonomy (in this case, the
2015 US GAAP namespace), while the last one has a different
prefix, t. It was created by AT&T with their own namespace. Also,

note that only concepts with the monetary time have a balance. Also see the first concept, which has the text block type from the data type registry, as opposed to the others that use data types from the original XBRL specification (xbrli prefix).

Concept	Type	Period type	Balance
us-gaap:FairValueByBalanceSheetGroupingTextBlock	nonnum:textBlockItemType	duration	–
us-gaap:ShortTermInvestments	xbrli:monetaryItemType	instant	debit
us-gaap:IncomeLossFromDiscontinuedOperationsNetOfTax	xbrli:monetaryItemType	duration	credit
us-gaap:WeightedAverageNumberOfSharesOutstandingBasic	xbrli:sharesItemType	duration	–
t:SubsequentEventNumberOfTowersSubjectToFailedSaleLeaseBack	xbrli:integerItemType	instant	–

Figure 3.9: Some examples of concepts and their type, period type and balance from the US GAAP taxonomy.

3.8 Metrics in the Data Point Model (DPM)

DPM-based taxonomies (European Banking Authority, ...) have different conventions on the usage of concepts than the examples given in this Chapter.

In EDGAR filings and the like (which we call presentation-based taxonomies as will become clear in Chapter 5), concepts represent real-world concepts, such as the assets of a company or the taxes paid.

While everything we are introducing in this chapter also applies to DPM-based taxonomies, the latter add an extra layer of semantics, and use concepts in a more abstract way. First, the DPM architecture documents use the word "metrics" rather than "concept"[4].

3.8.1 Naming conventions

In DPM-based taxonomies, metrics SQNames are not meant to be human readable. They look like the obscure `eba_met:eba_mi7`, `eba_met:eba_si7`, `es_met:es_bd3`, where the letters carry information on ownership of metrics as well as types, e.g., `m` for a monetary type. This is a DPM-specific convention that goes beyond the XBRL standard, in which SQNames are blackboxes[5].

---

[4]The DPM architectures documents also use the word "concept," but do so in a much broader sense than we do, which also includes other kinds of report elements that will be introduced later in this book. This is also consistent with the XBRL specifications, but is really a syntactic detail that end users should be shielded from. We thus recommend using the word "concept" as in this book, while having in mind that the DPM uses the word "metrics" instead and that XBRL specifications would call it something along the lines of "non-abstract item" or "non-abstract primary item".

[5]Note that EDGAR filings also have a specific convention on concept names: all SQNames are human-readable, which also goes beyond the XBRL standard

In DPM-based taxonomies, metrics only have real-world semantics meaning alongside dimensions. Hypercubes and dimensions are
described in Chapter 7.

3.8.2   Recommendations for the DPM learning curve

In general, from a pedagogical perspective, we highly recommend
first learning, and understanding, XBRL with EDGAR filings or
similar taxonomies (we call them presentation-based), and looking
at DPM taxonomies only in a second step. Getting acquainted
with the DPM architecture is much easier when one already has
a basic understanding of all the XBRL building blocks, because
it then comes down to learning different usage conventions and to
mapping terminology, such as knowing that DPM metrics are concepts with obscure names, that DPM concepts are report elements
that include DPM metrics and dimensions, and so on.

For this pedagogical reason, the architecture of this book is
highly focused on presentation-based taxonomies, even though we
regularly point out to what is specific to the DPM architecture.

3.9   XML syntax of an XBRL taxonomy schema

In order to define taxonomy schemata, which are dictionaries of
concepts, XBRL leverages the XML Schema standard. A taxonomy
schema is, in terms of syntax, an XML Schema.

3.9.1   XML Schema

XML Schema is a W3C standard that supports validation of XML
documents in a way more powerful than the Document Type Definitions (DTD) that can appear in XML documents. XML Schema
supports namespaces, QNames, complex structures, a core set of

builtin data types that can be extended. Any developer dealing with taxonomy schemata on the syntactic level should be familiar with XML Schema. We thus recommend reading a book that explains it in more depth, especially on how to declare elements that have a simple type.

In summary, an XBRL instance is an XML document and each taxonomy schema in the DTS (see Section 3.2.4) is an XML Schema document. The XBRL instance is valid against the set of taxonomy schemata in the DTS in the sense of the XML Schema standard.

More exactly, there is:

- a special builtin XML Schema document that describes the core of XBRL and that corresponds to the namespace associated with the `xbrli` prefix. This schema can be found at `http://www.xbrl.org/2003/xbrl-instance-2003-12-31.xsd`.

- a few more XML Schema documents that describes the additional types and units defined in this chapter (`num` and `nonnum` prefixes). These schemata can be found at `http://www.xbrl.org/dtr/type/nonNumeric-2009-12-16.xsd` and `http://www.xbrl.org/dtr/type/numeric-2009-12-16.xsd`. As you can see from the dates, they were designed almost six years later.

- as many XML Schema documents as there are concept (or user-defined type) namespaces in the DTS. This is because each XML Schema document defines all its elements in its target namespace. Figure 3.10 shows how a taxonomy schema typically looks like.

Element declarations are described in details in Section 3.9.3. Binding the schemata to the instance is explained in Section 3.9.4.

```
<?xml version="1.0"?>
<xs:schema
    xmlns:xs="http://www.w3.org/2001/XMLSchema"
    targetNamespace="http://example.com/my-namespace">
  <xs:import .../>
  <xs:import .../>
  <xs:import .../>
  ...
  <xs:element .../>
  <xs:element .../>
  <xs:element .../>
  <xs:element .../>
  <xs:element .../>
  <xs:element .../>
  <xs:element .../>
  ...
</xs:schema>
```

Figure 3.10: The skeleton of a taxonomy schema, which is an XML Schema. The target namespace corresponds to the namespace of the concepts it defines. The concepts being defined are organized as a flat list of element declarations. It also imports further schemata (xbrli, ...) and binds more prefixes as needed.

The schema import machinery is described in details in Section 3.9.5.

The instance document as a whole – remember that many of the involved elements bear the xbrli prefix – is valid against the full set of schemata listed above. The xbrli:xbrl, xbrli:cont ext and xbrli:unit elements, as their prefixes indicate, are valid against element declarations found in this core schema, while each fact is valid against the corresponding element declaration (the one corresponding to the fact's concept) in its taxonomy schema (the one corresponding to the concept's namespace).

It is important to be aware that XML Schema validation is

required, but not enough to guarantee that an instance is also valid in the sense of XBRL semantics. An XBRL processor must not only make sure that the instance is valid against the core schema plus the DTS taxonomy schemata, but also that it fulfills the additional validity constraints of XBRL.

3.9.2 QNames

Before we dive into defining new concepts with XML Schema element declarations, we need to explain how their names are mapped to XML Schema.

In XBRL, concepts, units, types, etc, are identified by qualified names, also referred to as SQName in the Open Information Model. A qualified name is made of a prefix and a local name separated by a colon, such as `us-gaap:Assets`, as well as a (hidden) namespace that the prefix represents for convenience, in this case `http://fasb .org/us-gaap/2015-01-31`. The short rationale for this, which is also given in the Open Information Model draft, is that, otherwise, one would have to use literals similar to the Clark notation, like `{http://fasb.org/us-gaap/2015-01-31} Assets`. This would be very fastidious to both read and write.

QNames vs. SQNames

In the underlying XML syntax, these qualified names are directly mapped to XML's QNames. QNames, just like SQNames, are made of a local name, a prefix and a namespace and the prefix acts as a proxy to a namespace. However, there are two differences between SQNames and QNames:

- The local name in a QName must be an NCName. For example, it may not begin with a digit. SQNames allow a larger subset of local names, which is convenient for referring to companies with their CIK, for example. This difference is of

no practical importance for concepts, units and types because
the stricter requirements of QNames apply to them anyway.

- The prefix of a QName may be bound to different namespaces at different places of even the same XML document.
  The SQName framework requires that a prefix is bound to
  the same namespace within the same XBRL report, which
  allows comparing qualified names keeping namespaces out of
  the picture. We strongly recommend sticking to this stricter
  SQName convention and use prefixes consistently within an
  XBRL report. We furthermore strongly recommend to stick
  to the same prefixes across reports whenever applicable, as
  is common practice in the XBRL community. For example,
  xbrli should be consistently bound with the XBRL instance,
  so that all builtin types can use it. The same applies to using
  the us-gaap prefix for the US GAAP taxonomy (regardless
  of the year), etc.

Prefix bindings

In the XML syntax, whenever a QName is used, whether it is a
concept name, a data type or a unit, its prefix must be bound to
a namespace using an xmlns attribute, as described in the XML
Names specification. For example, the attribute xmlns:xbrli="h
ttp://www.xbrl.org/2003/instance" associates the prefix xbrli
with the URI http://www.xbrl.org/2003/instance in all the de-
scendant nodes of the containing XML element.

We assume that the reader of this section knows how this machinery works, and otherwise refer to the W3C XML Names specification, or to a book on XML. Throughout this book, we take care
of binding prefixes in each XML document or element shown as an
example, so that each example is standalone. We also provide tables that summarize commonly used bindings and refer to QNames

using only commonly used prefixes, having these bindings in mind. We recommend using these bindings as well.

3.9.3 Concept definitions

We saw in Section 2.8 that each fact is described with an XML element. This XML element bears the name of the concept against which the fact is reported (see Figure 3.11a).

A concept such as, in this example, us-gaap:Assets, can be declared in an XML Schema using an XML Schema element declaration (see Figure 3.11b).

Each element declaration that introduces a new concept must be in the substitution group of a special, abstract element declaration named xbrli:item. The latter is defined in the core XBRL schema (xbrli prefix).

A very quick summary of the syntax for defining new concepts is that the qualified name (SQName) of the concept corresponds to the name (QName) of the element declaration, and the data type of the concept corresponds to the XML Schema type of the element declaration. Further attributes with the xbrli correspond to the period type and balance.

Hence, the XML element that describes the fact is valid against the element declaration that describes its concept. The validation of the fact against the period type and balance of the concept, however, is outside the scope of XML Schema and is performed as part of some complementary XBRL validation machinery that any XBRL processor is required to perform.

Let us now go more in details on how the properties of the element declaration map to the properties of concepts that we have described in this chapter.

```
<us-gaap:Assets
    xmlns:us-gaap="http://fasb.org/us-gaap/2015-01-31"
    contextRef="cocacola-in-april"
    unitRef="dollars"
    decimals="-6">
  91016000000
</us-gaap:Assets>
```

(a) A fact as an XML element, which uses the concept's qualified name,
us-gaap:Assets, as its name. It appears in the XBRL instance document, which is an XML file.

```
<xs:element
    xmlns:xs="http://www.w3.org/2001/XMLSchema"
    xmlns:xbrli="http://www.xbrl.org/2003/instance"
    name="Assets"
    type="xbrli:monetaryItemType"
    xbrli:periodType="instant"
    xbrli:balance="debit"              Concept metadata
    abstract="false"
    nillable="true"
    substitutionGroup="xbrli:item"/>
```

(b) An element declaration which defines the concept us-gaap:Assets.
It appears in an XBRL taxonomy schema, which is an XML Schema file.

Figure 3.11: A fact in an XBRL instance (XML document), and the
corresponding concept definition in the taxonomy schema (XML
Schema document). Only the local name of the concept is specified, because the namespace is the same across an entire taxonomy
schema.

Concept name

The qualified name of the concept is also the name of the element being declared. Remember that we said that all concepts within the same taxonomy schema share the same namespace. Hence, element declarations only specify the local name of their QName in the name attribute – its namespace is implicit as being the target namespace of the schema in which it appears.

Hence, in the current example, "Assets" is used as a name and the US GAAP namespace is implicit and is the target namespace of the US GAAP taxonomy schema. It is in theory optional for the taxonomy schema to have a target namespace, but we strongly advise against omitting it as it significantly reduces interoperability. Instead, it is advisable to use a target namespace with a host that you have control on, for example if you own the domain example.com, your target namespace should be something like

http://www.example.com/my-taxonomy/2015

or, for US GAAP concepts for the year 2015:

http://fasb.org/us-gaap/2015-01-31

Figure 3.12 shows how the target namespace for the `Assets` is defined for the entire taxonomy schema.

```
<?xml version="1.0"?>
<xs:schema
    xmlns:xs="http://www.w3.org/2001/XMLSchema"
    xmlns:xbrli="http://www.xbrl.org/2003/instance"
    targetNamespace="http://fasb.org/us-gaap/2015-01-31">

    <!-- some more machinery to import the xbrli schema -->

    <xs:element
      name="Assets"
      type="xbrli:monetaryItemType"
      xbrli:periodType="instant"
      xbrli:balance="debit"
      nillable="true"
      abstract="false"
      substitutionGroup="xbrli:item"/>

    <!-- ... more element declarations -->

</xs:schema>
```

Figure 3.12: An element declaration in its XML Schema file, with a target namespace. The machinery to import the xbrli schema was omitted for now.

Data type

The type attribute, which is in no namespace and is a standard XML Schema attribute, refers to the chosen data type, as its entire QName. The prefix needs to be bound in the schema with the classical XML Namespace machinery. Also, if you use the predefined data types shown in this chapter, you need to import their schemata accordingly.

The main XBRL instance schema, which contains all xbrli-prefixed types, is available under

http://www.xbrl.org/2003/xbrl-instance-2003-12-31.xsd

This schema must be imported in any case, except if you do not make any use of the xbrli prefix in concept types — if you define your own concepts, though, you will need this prefix.

The schema for additional numeric types (with prefix `num`) is available under

> `http://www.xbrl.org/dtr/type/numeric-2009-12-16.xsd`

and that for additional non-numeric types (with prefix `nonnum`) under

> `http://www.xbrl.org/dtr/type/nonNumeric-2009-12-16.xsd`

You can import a schema with an `xs:import` element right under the `xs:schema` root element, as shown on Figure 3.13.

Most XBRL processors keep these schemata in a cache to avoid downloading them every time.

Period type and balance

The element declaration for a concept contains a few more attributes defined in the core `xbrli` schema. The `xbrli:periodType` attribute specifies the period type for the concept being defined, and contains either the value "duration" or "instant". The `xbrli:balance` attribute specifies the balance for the concept being defined, and contains either the value "credit" or "debit".

These two attributes have no semantics in XML Schema and must be processed by an XBRL processor on top of it.

Nillable concepts

The `nillable` attribute, which in no namespace, can be set to "true" or "false" in order to allow or disallow xml:nil values to be reported. The semantics of this attribute is covered by XML Schema.

```
<?xml version="1.0"?>
<xs:schema
    xmlns:xs="http://www.w3.org/2001/XMLSchema"
    xmlns:xbrli="http://www.xbrl.org/2003/instance"
    targetNamespace="http://fasb.org/us-gaap/2015-01-31">

  <xs:import
    namespace="http://www.xbrl.org/2003/instance"
    schemaLocation=
      "http://www.xbrl.org/2003/xbrl-instance-2003-12-31.xsd"/>

  <xs:element
    name="Assets"
    type="xbrli:monetaryItemType"
    abstract="false"
    nillable="true"
    xbrli:balance="debit"
    substitutionGroup="xbrli:item"
    xbrli:periodType="instant"/>

</xs:schema>
```

Figure 3.13: An element declaration using a type, and importing the schema defining that type.

Additional underlying machinery

Finally, a few other XML Schema attributes are required, but are always the same for defining new concepts in the sense of this chapter.

The `abstract` attribute (no namespace) must be set to "false" in order for facts to be allowed to report values against this concept. It can also be omitted, which is equivalent.

The `substitutionGroup` attribute (no namespace) must be set to "xbrli:item"

We will see in later chapter other element declarations with different `abstract` or `substitutionGroup` attribute values, but these have completely different semantics. We refer to the XML Schema specification for more details on substitution groups, however this knowledge is not at all necessary to create taxonomy schemata.

3.9.4 Binding instances to taxonomy schemata

Now that we have all pieces of an XBRL taxonomy schema in place, let us explore how it, and other schemata, can be linked to the XBRL instance that uses its concepts.

The dual machinery

There are two mechanisms that exist in parallel for linking instances to taxonomy schemata:

1. On the lower XML Schema level, with a `xsi:schemaLocation` attribute[6]. This level is ignored by XBRL, even though we highly recommend to add schema locations with this attribute so that the instance can be validated with XML Schema processors that rely on these hints in an inter-operable way. This machinery is standardized and well documented in XML Schema literature.

2. On the upper XBRL level, with a simple link from the instance to the taxonomy schema. This is the official way that the DTS is resolved by an XBRL processor.

We advise extreme care in ensuring that these two machineries co-exist in a consistent way, that is, that the referenced XML Schema files are the same. This is because many XBRL processors do rely on XML Schema libraries for the schema resolution in addition to following the XBRL linking machinery. Conflicts between the two machineries could result in errors.

We now explain both machineries.

---

[6]This is for schemata with a target namespace. We stated earlier that it is strongly recommended to always define concepts in a namespace.

The xsi:schemaLocation attribute

The `xsi:schemaLocation` attribute is the official XML Schema
way of linking an instance to one or several schemata.

The XML Schema specification states that XML documents
may bear their own hints on the location of schemata. For schemata
that have a namespace, this is done with a `xsi:schemaLocation`
attribute.

This attribute contains a value that is typed as a list of strings.
In terms of syntax, it simply means that its value is a string literal
that contains URIs that are separated by spaces. These URIs go
two by two: A namespace URI, then the URI (actually URL) of its
physical location, then another namespace URI, the URI (URL) of
its physical location, and so on, with any namespaces as desired.

If we take our typical example of instance shown on Figure 2.11,
we can augment it with a `xsi:schemaLocation` attribute as shown
on Figure 3.14. In this case, we need two schemata: the core `xbrli`
schema, as well as the schema that contains the concept definitions
for the US GAAP namespace. This schema actually exists over
the Web, but here we are assuming that we defined it ourselves
as shown on Figure 3.13, in a file stored next to our instance,
taxonomy.xsd.

```
<?xml version="1.0"?>
<xbrli:xbrl
    xmlns:xsi="http://www.w3.org/2001/XMLSchema-instance"
    xmlns:xbrli="http://www.xbrl.org/2003/instance"
    xmlns:us-gaap="http://fasb.org/us-gaap/2015-01-31"
    xmlns:ISO4217="http://www.xbrl.org/2003/iso4217"

    xsi:schemaLocation="

      http://www.xbrl.org/2003/instance
      http://www.xbrl.org/2003/xbrl-instance-2003-12-31.xsd

      http://fasb.org/us-gaap/2015-01-31
      taxonomy.xsd              XML Schema machinery

    ">
  <xbrli:context id="cocacola-in-april">
    <xbrli:entity>
      <xbrli:identifier scheme="http://www.sec.gov/CIK">
        0000021344 <!-- This would be Coca Cola -->
      </xbrli:identifier>
    </xbrli:entity>
    <xbrli:period>
      <xbrli:instant>2015-04-03</xbrli:instant>
    </xbrli:period>
  </xbrli:context>
  <xbrli:unit id="dollars">
    <xbrli:measure>
      ISO4217:USD
    </xbrli:measure>
  </xbrli:unit>
  <us-gaap:Assets
      contextRef="cocacola-in-april"
      unitRef="dollars"
      decimals="-6">
    91016000000
  </us-gaap:Assets>
</xbrli:xbrl>
```

Figure 3.14: A complete XBRL instance that points to a taxonomy schema. This example uses the XML Schema location machinery. The `xsi:schemaLocation` is ignored by XBRL, yet recommended to have for interoperability.

```
<link:schemaRef
    xmlns:link="http://www.xbrl.org/2003/linkbase"
    xmlns:xlink="http://www.w3.org/1999/xlink"
    xlink:href="http://www.example.com/taxonomy.xsd"
    xlink:type="simple" />
```

Figure 3.15: A simple link, in this case a reference to a taxonomy schema.

XLink and Simple links

XBRL does not rely on the above `xsi:schemaLocation` attribute. Instead, it uses what are called simple links to the taxonomy schemata of which it uses the concepts. The technology behind these links is a W3C standard known as XLink.

In XLink, there are two kinds of links: simple links and extended links. We are leaving extended links aside for now, and focus on simple links.

A simple link simply points to a document, or to a specific place in a document. It is a bit like an HTML link. Figure 3.15 shows a simple link to a taxonomy schema.

From a syntactic perspective, a simple link is an XML element with a few attributes. The XLink specification leaves it open how to name this element. In the case of a link to a schema though, XBRL requires that it is named `link:schemaRef`. The `link` prefix is associated with an XBRL-specific namespace shown on Figure 3.16. The other namespace used is the official XLink namespace.

A simple link, and in particular the `link:schemaRef` element, has two mandatory attributes that are standard XLink attributes, in the `xlink` namespace:

- `xlink:href` is the location (relative or absolute URL) of the taxonomy schema file– or of whatever the simple link points

Prefix	Namespace
link	http://www.xbrl.org/2003/linkbase
xlink	http://www.w3.org/1999/xlink

Figure 3.16: Namespaces and prefixes commonly used for simple links

to if it is not a schema reference.

- `xlink:type` must have the value "simple" to specify that this is a simple link.

All other optional XLink attributes can safely be ignored and have no semantics in XBRL.

However, it is worth mentioning the `xml:base` attribute, which allows you to tweak the meaning of relative URIs to your convenience. If you use a relative URI (as is the case in our example), then by default the base URI of the XBRL instance is taken to resolve these. This makes it easy to build simple link to a taxonomy schema located in the same folder as the XBRL instance, in which case it suffices to use the file name. The `xml:base` attribute allows you to modify this default behavior.

We refer to the XML Base specification for more specific details on this attribute.

The schema reference inside the instance

In order to bind an XBRL instance to one or several taxonomy schemata, one or several `link:schemaRef` simple links must be placed at the beginning of the instance document, as shown on Figure 3.17, which takes our example from Chapter 2.

The taxonomy schema, in turn, can import further taxonomy schemata using regular XML schema imports or includes. All the schemata in the transitive closure of these imports are added to the DTS.

For the sake of completeness, we also show on Figure 3.18 our XBRL instance linking to its DTS using both machineries: the `xsi:schemaLocation` attribute and the `link:schemaRef` simple link. This is what we recommend in practice.

3.9.5 Importing schemata from other schemata

Finally, we now show how the DTS graph can be built by connecting taxonomy schemata to further taxonomy schemata.

Linking taxonomy schemata to further taxonomy schemata is done using XML Schema machinery (import and include), and this machinery is used by XBRL as well. The use of redefine, though, is forbidden in XBRL.

As explained in Section 3.2.4, XBRL has a mechanism for discovering all the taxonomy schemata by navigating from XML (Schema) file to XML (Schema) file, following all the links available. The so gathered DTS contains all the concepts used by the instance to report facts. The starting point for gathering up the DTS is the XBRL instance.

Figure 3.19 summarizes the DTS discovery on the syntactic level starting with the instance.

3.9.6 A complete example

A complete instance in the XML syntax can be downloaded online from the location provided in Section 1.5. This instance can be found under the samples for Chapter 3.

3.9.7 There is concept and concept

Before this chapter is closed, a few words have to be said on the use of the word "concept" for those who are going to take a look at

```
<?xml version="1.0"?>
<xbrli:xbrl
    xmlns:xbrli="http://www.xbrl.org/2003/instance"
    xmlns:us-gaap="http://fasb.org/us-gaap/2015-01-31"
    xmlns:ISO4217="http://www.xbrl.org/2003/iso4217"
    xmlns:link="http://www.xbrl.org/2003/linkbase"
    xmlns:xlink="http://www.w3.org/1999/xlink" >
    <link:schemaRef
      xlink:href="taxonomy.xsd"
      xlink:type="simple" />      XBRL simple link machinery
    <xbrli:context id="cocacola-in-april">
      <xbrli:entity>
        <xbrli:identifier scheme="http://www.sec.gov/CIK">
          0000021344 <!-- This would be Coca Cola -->
        </xbrli:identifier>
      </xbrli:entity>
      <xbrli:period>
        <xbrli:instant>2015-04-03</xbrli:instant>
      </xbrli:period>
    </xbrli:context>

    <xbrli:unit id="dollars">
      <xbrli:measure>
        ISO4217:USD
      </xbrli:measure>
    </xbrli:unit>

    <us-gaap:Assets
        contextRef="cocacola-in-april"
        unitRef="dollars"
        decimals="-6">
      91016000000
    </us-gaap:Assets>

</xbrli:xbrl>
```

Figure 3.17: A complete XBRL instance that points to a taxonomy schema called taxonomy.xsd and located in the same directory as the instance. This example uses the XBRL simple link machinery.

```xml
<?xml version="1.0"?>
<xbrli:xbrl
    xmlns:xsi="http://www.w3.org/2001/XMLSchema-instance"
    xmlns:xbrli="http://www.xbrl.org/2003/instance"
    xmlns:us-gaap="http://fasb.org/us-gaap/2015-01-31"
    xmlns:ISO4217="http://www.xbrl.org/2003/iso4217"

    xsi:schemaLocation="

      http://www.xbrl.org/2003/instance
      http://www.xbrl.org/2003/xbrl-instance-2003-12-31.xsd

      http://fasb.org/us-gaap/2015-01-31
      taxonomy.xsd

    ">                              XML Schema machinery
  <link:schemaRef
    xlink:href="taxonomy.xsd"
    xlink:type="simple" />   XBRL simple link machinery

  <xbrli:context id="cocacola-in-april">
    <xbrli:entity>
      <xbrli:identifier scheme="http://www.sec.gov/CIK">
        0000021344 <!-- This would be Coca Cola -->
      </xbrli:identifier>
    </xbrli:entity>
    <xbrli:period>
      <xbrli:instant>2015-04-03</xbrli:instant>
    </xbrli:period>
  </xbrli:context>

  <xbrli:unit id="dollars">
    <xbrli:measure>
      ISO4217:USD
    </xbrli:measure>
  </xbrli:unit>

  <us-gaap:Assets
      contextRef="cocacola-in-april"
      unitRef="dollars"
      decimals="-6">
    91016000000
  </us-gaap:Assets>

</xbrli:xbrl>
```

Figure 3.18: A complete XBRL instance that points to a taxonomy schema using both the standard XML Schema machinery and the XBRL simple link machinery. The `xsi:schemaLocation` is ignored by XBRL, yet recommended to have for interoperability.

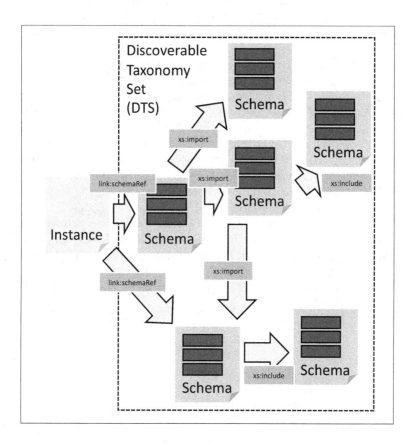

Figure 3.19: A discoverable taxonomy set as a DAG of taxonomy schemata. The mechanisms with which the edges of this DAG are constructed syntactically are shown.

any XBRL specification. In this chapter, we introduced the notion of a concept in a way that is semantically relevant to reporting: "what" a fact reports. This is also the definition that Charles Hoffman advocates for in everyday usage.

In the raw XBRL specification though, the word "concept" is also used for many other building blocks than those described in this chapter. XBRL concepts are in two categories: the first one is called XBRL items (yes, this would be the substitution group used above) and the second one is called XBRL tuples. What we call a concept in this chapter is a concrete XBRL item, that is, an element declaration in the substitution group of xbrli:item, and with an abstract attribute set to false — these are the ones against which values can actually be reported.

It is important that this be said in order for the reader to have this in mind when looking at the XBRL specifications. Throughout this book, we will stick to calling concepts what has been defined in this chapter, and will use a different wording for the building blocks: "report elements", that will be introduced later on. It should very soon become clear that this simplifies the understanding of XBRL a lot.

Chapter 4

Labels

When facts have been reported and validated against concept metadata, they need to be displayed to end users. A lot of the XBRL machinery is geared towards presenting the data in a way that users understand, and without IT knowledge.

The first step towards user-friendliness is to display concepts in the user's own language, both in terms of the language they speak, and in terms of shielding them from all the technical complexity.

4.1 User-friendliness

In XBRL, concepts are referred to with internal names known as qualified names, as explained in Section 3.3. A qualified name looks like `us-gaap:Assets`. Many business users that are a bit tech-savvy are aware of them and see them as the "names with the colon in the middle." They are happy to use them when they communicate with software developers or sometimes even between them.

However, it is hard to imagine that a company would produce a fancy-looking annual fiscal report in PDF or printed form, and present it to their investors, using these names. Firstly, because these names are usually made of English words and reports are produced in many other languages, secondly because it can be confusing to most people — and it would be foolish to require anybody who reads a fiscal report to know about XBRL — and third but no less important, because it absolutely does not look good.

In this chapter, we will see how concepts can be associated with user-friendly labels, how these labels can vary with the context in which a fact is displayed, and how labels can be provided in several languages.

4.2 More on the DTS

In Chapter 3, we introduced the concept of Discoverable Taxonomy Set (DTS). While the instance has the data, the associated DTS has the metadata.

4.2.1 Taxonomy linkbases

In Section 3.2.4, we introduced one component of the DTS: the taxonomy schema, which is a flat list of concepts on the logical level. The other component of the DTS is made of taxonomy linkbases. On the logical level, the taxonomy linkbases simply form a big graph. This graph as a whole is very heterogeneous though, so that it makes sense to split into semantically meaningful sub-graphs.

4.2.2 The label linkbase

One of these sub-graphs is called the label linkbase. A label linkbase is a bipartite graph that associates concepts (those of the taxonomy schema) with labels. A label has a language and a label role.

Each edge connects a concept to a label. One concept may be associated with several labels with varying languages and label roles.

Figure 4.1 shows an example of label linkbase with 3 concepts and 5 labels.

In the next two sections, we now go into more details on languages and label roles.

4.3 Label languages

Labels can appear in multiple languages. Each label is associated to a given concept and stamped with a language. Languages are typically defined using codes from RFC 1766, such as en, en-GB, en-US, fr, or de-CH. The language codes (en, fr, de, ...) are defined in ISO 639, while country codes are defined in ISO 3166 (GB, US, ...). New standards for language codes are also on their way (IETF).

Figure 4.2 shows some of the most used language codes.

4.4 Label roles

Labels can have multiple roles. Roles give the flexibility to display a fact's concept depending on the rendering context. For example, if a fact is displayed alone, the label used should be a bit more verbose. If on the other side the fact is displayed with 100 others, nicely arranged, a more terse label will do.

4.4.1 Universal Resource Identifiers

A label role is a URI. We will see later that the usage of URIs to identify resources are common in XBRL. A URI looks like a URL such as the one used in Web browsers, except that they will mostly not resolve to any website. They are more like a naming scheme that everybody agrees on to identify resources. In XBRL, most URIs actually use the HTTP scheme, however some URIs can also be bound that use the urn scheme instead.

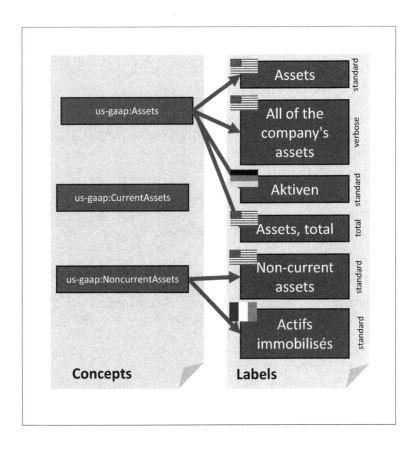

Figure 4.1: A label linkbase, which is a bipartite graph. Each edge connects a concept with a label. Each label is annotated with a language and a role.

Code	Language	Country
de	German	
de-AT	German	Austria
de-CH	German	Switzerland
de-DE	German	Germany
en	English	
en-GB	English	United Kingdom
en-US	English	United States of America
es	Spanish	
fr	French	
fr-CH	French	Switzerland
fr-FR	French	France
it	Italian	
ja	Japanese	
zh	Chinese	

Figure 4.2: A few examples of language codes

All standardized label roles use the HTTP scheme and begin with `http://www.xbrl.org/2003/`

4.4.2 Verbosity

Label verbosity provides three levels: terse (short), normal (standard), verbose (extended). The label role URIs are shown on Figure 4.3. The standard label role is the default if no label role is specified.

4.4.3 Sign

Some concepts, especially in accounting, can be associated in a fact to negative or positive values. An example is for reporting income or loss. For example, Coca Cola reported a fact against the concept

Verbosity	Label Role
Terse	http://www.xbrl.org/2003/terseLabel
Normal	http://www.xbrl.org/2003/label
Verbose	http://www.xbrl.org/2003/verboseLabel

Figure 4.3: A list of label roles related to verbosity.

Sign	Label Role
+	http://www.xbrl.org/2003/role/positiveLabel
-	http://www.xbrl.org/2003/role/negativeLabel
0	http://www.xbrl.org/2003/role/zeroLabel

Figure 4.4: A list of label roles related to sign.

us-gaap:OtherNonoperatingIncomeExpense with the value of $ -1,263,000,000 for the fiscal year 2013. When reported as is, that is, negative, the standard label is "Other Nonoperating Income (Expense)." In other words, it is an income of $ -1,263,000,000. But, equivalently, one could say that it is an expense of $ 1,263,000,000. XBRL makes it possible by using a negative label such as "Other Nonoperating Expense." If the fact had been known to be positive, it could also be displayed as "Other Nonoperating Income."

There are three standardized label role URIs for adapting the label to the sign of the value associated with the concept, be it positive, negative, or zero, as shown on Figure 4.4.

It is crucial to understand that the fact stays identical, and only the way it is presented to the user changes. If a negative label is chosen, the sign of the value is to be inverted for presentation to the business user — even if the fact value turns out to actually be positive, in which case the value will be displayed as negative (e.g., a profit of $8,634,000,000 is the same as a loss of $ -8,634,000,000).

Finally, there exist six more label role URIs that combine the

Sign	Verbosity	Label Role
+	terse	http://www.xbrl.org/2003/role/positiveTerseLabel
-	terse	http://www.xbrl.org/2003/role/negativeTerseLabel
0	terse	http://www.xbrl.org/2003/role/zeroTerseLabel
+	verbose	http://www.xbrl.org/2003/role/positiveVerboseLabel
-	verbose	http://www.xbrl.org/2003/role/negativeVerboseLabel
0	verbose	http://www.xbrl.org/2003/role/zeroVerboseLabel

Figure 4.5: A list of label roles related to sign and verbosity.

above three label roles with the a terse or verbose level of verbosity. They are shown on Figure 4.5.

4.4.4 Aggregations

When a fact is displayed as the total of other facts, the concept can be shown accordingly as being a total. For example, us-gaap: Assets is associated with the standard label role "Assets", but when it is displayed as a total, it can be shown instead as "TOTAL ASSETS."

A total label can be specified with the following label role URI: http://www.xbrl.org/2003/role/totalLabel

Another common use case in accounting, mostly found in cash flow statements, is when there is an initial value associated with a concept C, followed by a variation of this value over some time, followed by the resulting end value associated with that same concept C — but with a different period.

In this case, even though it is the same concept, the labels used will typically be different. For example, the concept us-gaap: CashAndCashEquivalentsAtCarryingValue, associated normally with the standard label "Cash and Cash Equivalents, at Carrying Value," will be displayed either as "Balance at beginning of year" or as "Balance at end of year."

Timeline	Label Role
Start	http://www.xbrl.org/2003/role/periodStartLabel
End	http://www.xbrl.org/2003/role/periodEndLabel

Figure 4.6: The label roles for starting and ending periods.

The two label role URIs for defining start and end labels are shown on Figure 4.6.

4.4.5 Miscellaneous information on the concept

Some more labels are not per se intended to be used in lieu of the concept name in presentation, but are here for documentation purposes, and for supporting the users of the taxonomy for reporting facts against the concept, and for arranging the concept amongst other concepts.

General documentation about the concept (its meaning, etc) can be made available with the label role URI `http://www.xbrl.org/2003/role/documentation`.

Some more label roles provide more fine-grained documentation regarding concepts, but their usage is much less common than the label roles shown until here. However, we provide them for the sake of completeness.

The definition itself of the concept can be associated with the label role URI `http://www.xbrl.org/2003/role/definitionGuidance`.

When a reporting authority requires, say, companies to submit filings, they may enforce that some concepts are mandatory to report, or just recommended. Alternatively, it may only be common practice[1] to do so, or the concept may only be required for com-

---

[1]This is the wording of the XBRL specification. Throughout this book, we will encourage usage of common practice. We are careful to not use the expression "best practice," as it would imply that deviating would be wrong.

pleteness with regard to other concepts. The label role URI to
specify this is `http://www.xbrl.org/2003/role/disclosureGui
dance`.

Facts reporting against different concepts are often displayed
together (for example, grouped in a balance sheet), as will be shown
in Chapter 5. Guidance regarding how a concept should be handled
in these renderings can be provided with the label role URI `http:
//www.xbrl.org/2003/role/presentationGuidance`.

In addition to defining the meaning of a concept, it is also crucial to explain *how* the value reported against this concept should
be measured or acquired. This guidance can be provided with the
label role URI `http://www.xbrl.org/2003/role/measurementGu
idance`.

Miscellaneous further comments can be provided with `http:
//www.xbrl.org/2003/role/commentaryGuidance`.

A concrete example of fact or value reported against the concept
can be provided with the label role URI `http://www.xbrl.org
/2003/role/exampleGuidance`.

4.5 So many label roles?

Even though there are lots of different standard label roles (22),
in most XBRL taxonomies, concepts are not typically associated
with so many labels. The average report uses 1, 2, sometimes 3 or
4 label roles for each concept: Usually a standard label, sometimes
a terse label, and when needed sign, total or period labels.

As far as languages are concerned, this varies depending on the
country. Anglophone countries typically only use the English language only (en, en-US or en-GB), while non-Anglophone countries
such as Japan use the local language as well as English. Multilin-

---

In XBRL, common practice is important because the more everybody sticks
to the same principles, the easier it gets to analyze reports.

gual countries such as Switzerland will typically use all their local languages (in this case German, French and Italian), plus English.

4.6   XML syntax of a label linkbase

So far, we have introduced the syntax for an XBRL instance for describing facts, as well as the syntax for XBRL taxonomy schemata, for describing concepts. There is one more, very big, piece to the puzzle: XBRL taxonomy linkbases. Labels are defined and associated to concepts using taxonomy linkbases, and subsequent chapters will also rely on them dramatically.

4.6.1   XBRL taxonomy linkbases

The syntax of XBRL taxonomy linkbases is very complex, much more than that of instances or taxonomy schemata. The involved machinery relies on XLink, a W3C specification that supports linking across XML documents.

We already introduced a bit of XLink in Section 3.9.4: simple links are used to assemble the DTS by linking instances to schemata and, as we will see, instances to linkbases, schemata to linkbases, linkbases to schemata.

A linkbase itself relies on another bit of the XLink technology, called extended links.

Yet, do not be daunted by what "complexity" means here. XBRL taxonomy linkbases, on the logical level, are much less complicated than their underlying extended link syntax: they are nothing else than graphs, and these graphs, in the XBRL world, are also called networks. The edges of these graphs are called relationships. The nodes are concepts, or labels, or other kinds of resources. If you think of linkbases as graphs, and of extended links as nothing more than a syntax to describe them, you will be alright.

So, if you lack knowledge of graph theory, it is very advisable to brush up a bit on nodes, edges, bipartite graphs, DAGs, trees, cycles, and so on. An abstract understanding of them will bring you much quicker to truly understanding XBRL taxonomy linkbases, than trying to fight your way through the XLink syntax.

As we saw in Section 4.2.2, in the case of a label linkbase, the graph is a bipartite graph that associates concepts to resources – in this case the resources are the labels. Each edge links a concept to a label. And each label is annotated with its language and label role, as described earlier in this chapter. If you understand this, you understood everything – all the rest is pure syntactic machinery.

Later in this book, we will introduce several other kinds of linkbases – some of the underlying graphs will only have concepts, some will also have resources, some will be bipartite, some will be directed acyclic graphs (DAGs), some will even be trees. But the syntax behind it is the same.

4.6.2   XML namespaces relevant to linkbases

There are two namespaces used in XBRL linkbases, as shown on Figure 4.7, associated with the prefixes `xlink` and `link`.

The `xlink` namespace corresponds to the XLink standard. Attributes in this namespace bear the linking semantics. The `link` namespace is standardized by XBRL, which defines the elements that are wearing the XLink outfit.

The `xsi` namespace is the standard XML Schema instance schema and is only used to bind taxonomy linkbases to their standard schema.

4.6.3   Graphs: Extended links

When a taxonomy designer or a filer defines their labels and associates them with their respective concepts, they will typically put them all in the same XML document, which is called a label

Prefix	Namespace
link	http://www.xbrl.org/2003/linkbase
xlink	http://www.w3.org/1999/xlink
xsi	http://www.w3.org/2001/XMLSchema-instance

Figure 4.7: Namespaces and prefixes commonly used in linkbases

linkbase, and which is a special case of taxonomy linkbase. Actually, each kind of taxonomy linkbase, in a taxonomy, has its own XML file.

All taxonomy linkbase documents, not only label linkbases, are XML documents that are valid against the schema located at the URL `http://www.xbrl.org/2003/xbrl-linkbase-2003-12-31.xsd`. This schema defines the linkbase elements in the `link` namespace, for example label links.

As can be seen on Figure 4.8, a linkbase has a `link:linkbase` root element[2]. This root element acts as a container. Inside it, there are extended link elements. In the case of a label linkbase, these are `link:labelLink` elements.

The `link:linkbase` element further contains an attribute with the name `xsi:schemaLocation`. It is optional and binds the taxonomy linkbase to its schema (always the standard XBRL linkbase schema).

As a side-note: an XBRL processor should, and most of them actually do, avoid loading the linkbase schema (or any other schema) from the `xbrl.org` or `w3.org` servers every time a linkbase is processed, but should cache it instead. This is especially important if XBRL usage scales up, because requests repeatedly coming from all over the world are a lot to handle and have costs. By caching, you are are being nice to both XBRL international and the W3C

---

[2]As explained before, we do not comment any further on the namespace bindings and assume that you are familiar with how they work.

```
<?xml version="1.0"?>
<link:linkbase
    xmlns:link="http://www.xbrl.org/2003/linkbase"
    xmlns:xlink="http://www.w3.org/1999/xlink"
    xsi:schemaLocation="
    http://www.xbrl.org/2003/linkbase
    http://www.xbrl.org/2003/xbrl-linkbase-2003-12-31.xsd
    ">
    <link:labelLink
        xlink:role="http://www.xbrl.org/2003/role/link"
        xlink:type="extended">
        <!-- the nodes and edges of the label linkbase graph -->
    </link:labelLink>                        Extended link

    <!-- more extended links -->

</link:linkbase>
```

Figure 4.8: The skeleton of a linkbase, in this case a label linkbase. Here, one extended link, which is a label link, is shown.

consortium, as well as to the other users.

The `link:labelLink` element has two required attributes.

You already know the `xlink:type` attribute, also used in simple links and introduced in Section 3.9.4. This attribute specifies whether the link is simple or extended. The `link:labelLink` is always extended.

`xlink:role` points to the so called role of the extended link. We will explain more in details what this means in Chapter 5 as we introduce other linkbases than label linkbases. For labels you can safely use the default role `http://www.xbrl.org/2003/role/link`, as is commonly done. This is common practice when concept labels are defined for the entire scope of the DTS.

Now, let us move on to the meat: the nodes and edges of the bipartite graph associating concepts with labels. All these nodes and edges are nested as a flat list inside extended link elements such as `link:labelLink`.

4.6.4   Nodes: Concept locators

The label linkbase is a bipartite graph. Some of the nodes are concepts, and some other are labels.

The concept nodes must point to concepts in the taxonomy schema, as we described them in Chapter 3. Concept nodes are called locators.

Figure 4.9 shows the syntax of a locator, and how it points to an existing concept declaration. `link:loc` elements are put inside extended link elements such as `link:labelLink` shown in the previous section.

A locator looks very much like a simple link to a concept declaration. Hence, its attributes are the same as the one we introduced for `link:schemaRef` elements, which allow instances to point to taxonomy schemata.

The `xlink:type` attribute must however have a value of "locator" instead of "simple".

The `xlink:href` attribute must not only point to the taxonomy schema file, but also use a URI fragment to point to the exact concept. To put it simple: each concept declaration must have an `id` attribute (which is the standard XML ID attribute), and the value of this attribute is added to the taxonomy schema file with a sharp in-between. In general, the `id` attribute has exactly the same value (with possibly a few uppercase/lowercase/underscore tweaks) as the local name of the concept and we recommend sticking to this convention. No collisions can happen, as all concepts declared in the same taxonomy schema share the same prefix – and as said earlier, we recommend always to use a prefix for concepts.

For more on customizing your own links, you can read the W3C XPointer recommendation, however in XBRL, locator links are as simple as described above and there is no need for any more complex machinery.

```
<xs:element
    xmlns:xs="http://www.w3.org/2001/XMLSchema"
    xmlns:xbrli="http://www.xbrl.org/2003/instance"
    id="assets"  ◄
    name="Assets"
    type="xbrli:monetaryItemType"
    abstract="false"
    nillable="true"
    xbrli:balance="debit"
    substitutionGroup="xbrli:item"
    xbrli:periodType="instant"/>              (points to)
```

(a) In the file **us-gaap-taxonomy.xsd**: the concept declaration from Chapter 3, to which an **id** attribute was added

```
<link:loc
    xmlns:link="http://www.xbrl.org/2003/linkbases"
    xmlns:xlink="http://www.w3.org/1999/xlink"
    xlink:type="locator"
    xlink:href="us-gaap-taxonomy.xsd#assets"
    xlink:label="us_gaap_assets"/>
```

(b) The locator, referring to the above ID in its **xlink:href** XPointer. It is assumed here that the label linkbase file is in the same directory as the taxonomy schema.

Figure 4.9: A locator, which is a simple link to a concept declaration in the taxonomy schema.

The last attribute, `xlink:label`, gives a name to the concept node so that edges of the same graph can be attached to it. It is not its label in the XBRL sense, only a reference that edges of the graph can use. A node's `xlink:label` is only local to the linkbase, and the value chosen is irrelevant in terms of XBRL semantics.

4.6.5   Nodes: (Label) resources

In the previous section, we built half of the nodes that constitute the label linkbase graph: these nodes point to concepts. The other half of the nodes are the labels that get associated with the concepts.

From an XLink viewpoint, labels are resources, and are defined with a `link:label` element. An example is shown on Figure 4.10.

Some of the attributes for label resources are already familiar: `xlink:label` identifies the resource as a node in such a way that edges can refer to it – again, `xlink:label` attributes are not to be confused with XBRL labels; their only use is to be bound with edges in the linkbase graph.

The `xlink:type` is also familiar. In the case of a label resource, it must be set to "resource."

Finally, the last two attributes identify the language and role of the label.

The language, as introduced in Section 4.3, can be specified with its code as a value of the `xml:lang` attribute. This attribute is a standard XML attribute.

The role, as introduced in Section 4.4, can be specified with its URI as a value of the `xlink:role` attribute.

The `link:label` element contains, as a child text node, the content of the label as a string. However, it is also allowed to embed some XHTML instead – in the latter case, the XHTML namespace must be correctly bound and used.

```
<link:label
      xmlns:link="http://www.xbrl.org/2003/linkbases"
      xmlns:xlink="http://www.w3.org/1999/xlink"
      xlink:type="resource"
      xlink:role="http://www.xbrl.org/2003/role/label"
      xlink:label="us_gaap_assets_label"
      xml:lang="en-US">
  Assets
</link:label>
```

Figure 4.10: A label resource. Its label role, language and caption are emphasized.

4.6.6 Edges: linking a locator to a resource

We now have all the nodes of our bipartite graph, the label linkbase, in place. We have on the one hand pointers to concepts – locators – and on the other hand labels – resources.

The last missing piece is the edges of this graph: each edge must bind a concept to a label. In XLink, edges are called arcs. The syntax is straightforward: there is one `link:labelArc` element for each edge, directly as a child of the `link:labelLinkbase` element. Figure 4.11 shows how such an arc.

Let us now go through the attributes of an arc element.

The attribute `xlink:type` was encountered before: it classifies XLink elements. In this case, it's an "arc".

The attributes `xlink:from` and `xlink:to` are the start point and end point of the edge: the graph is directed, hence edges are oriented. The values of these two attributes correspond to the desired concept locator or label resource, identified with their previously introduced `xlink:label` attributes.

Finally, the attribute `xlink:arcrole` is called an arc role URI and specifies what kind of arc this is. In the case of a label linkbase,

```
<link:loc
    xmlns:link="http://www.xbrl.org/2003/linkbases"
    xmlns:xlink="http://www.w3.org/1999/xlink"
    xlink:type="locator"
    xlink:href="us-gaap-taxonomy.xsd#assets"
    xlink:label="us_gaap_assets"/>
```

(a) A concept node.   (from)

```
<link:label
    xmlns:link="http://www.xbrl.org/2003/linkbases"
    xmlns:xlink="http://www.w3.org/1999/xlink"
    xlink:type="resource"
    xlink:role="http://www.xbrl.org/2003/role/label"
    xlink:label="us_gaap_assets_label"
    xml:lang="en-US">
Assets
</link:label>
```

(b) A label resource.   (to)

```
<link:labelArc
    xmlns:link="http://www.xbrl.org/2003/linkbases"
    xmlns:xlink="http://www.w3.org/1999/xlink"
    xlink:type="arc"
    xlink:from="us_gaap_assets"
    xlink:to="us_gaap_assets_label"
    xlink:arcrole=
      "http://www.xbrl.org/2003/arcrole/concept-label"/>
```

(c) An arc, i.e., an edge in the label linkbase graph.

Figure 4.11: An arc, connecting a concept node to a label resource. The three elements above (locator, label, arc) are direct children of the `link:labelLinkbase` element.

the arc role URI is always `http://www.xbrl.org/2003/arcrole/`
`concept-label`. We will encounter, later in this book, other kinds
of linkbases, and their edges will have different arc roles.

4.6.7 Wrap up on XLink attributes

We introduced a lot of attributes on the past few sections. Let us
now give a quick wrap up across all XLink elements.

`xlink:type` is common to locators, resources and arcs and,
surprise, has the value "locator", "resource" or "arc."

`xlink:label` (which is *not* an XBRL label!) stamps locators
and resources in a way that `xlink:to` and `xlink:from`, used on
arcs, can connect to them.

`xlink:href` allows a locator to point to a concept.

`xlink:role` and `xml:lang` stamp a label resource with a label
role and a language.

`xlink:arcrole` stamp a label arc with the appropriate arc role
URI common to all label linkbases.

Other optional attributes

We consciously skipped a few more XLink attributes that apply
to locator (`link:loc`), resource (e.g., for a label resource, `link:`
`label`) and arc elements (e.g., for a label arc, `link:labelArc`).
These are `xlink:title`, `xlink:show` and `xlink:actuate`.

These attributes have no special semantics within XBRL. We
refer to the XLink specification for more details on these.

4.6.8 Linking to a linkbase

We saw that the DTS is made of taxonomy schemata and of taxonomy linkbases. The DTS is made of the transitive closure of all the
linking machinery starting with the instance document. Figure 4.12
shows the possible links within a DTS: instance to schema, schema

to schema, instance to linkbase, schema to linkbase, linkbase to linkbase, linkbase to schema. We have already introduced the former two in Section 3.9.4 and 3.9.5.

From an instance

Linking to a taxonomy linkbase from an instance is done very similarly to linking to a taxonomy schema: with a simple link, as shown on Figure 4.13. This simple link must have the name `link:linkbaseRef`.

The `xlink:type` (simple) and `xlink:ref` (with the URL to the linkbase file) are the exact same as for schema references. Linkbase references have two more attributes.

The attribute `xlink:arcrole` must have the value `http://www.w3.org/1999/xlink/properties/linkbase`.

The optional attribute `xlink:role` specifies which kind of linkbase is referenced. It is a URI among the possible kinds of linkbases (so far, we only know label linkbases):

http://www.xbrl.org/2003/role/labelLinkbaseRef
http://www.xbrl.org/2003/role/presentationLinkbaseRef
http://www.xbrl.org/2003/role/calculationLinkbaseRef
http://www.xbrl.org/2003/role/definitionLinkbaseRef
http://www.xbrl.org/2003/role/referenceLinkbaseRef

If this attribute is omitted, the referenced linkbase may contain any kind of linkbase.

From a schema

Linking to a taxonomy linkbase from an schema is also done with a `link:linkbaseRef` element. This element is put in a special part of the schema, nested inside a `xs:annotation` and an `xs:appinfo` element, as shown on Figure 4.14. Many other XBRL machinery constructs also go into this appinfo location, as we will see later.

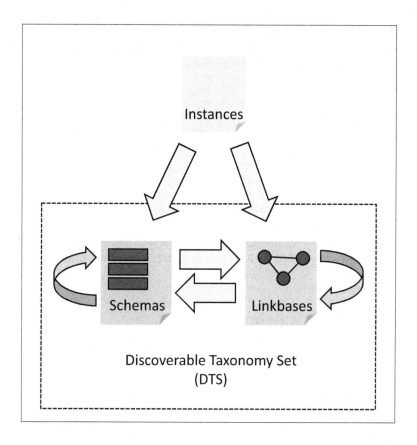

Figure 4.12: The link structure between elements of the DTS. Instances can point to schemata and linkbases. Schemata can point to other schemata or to linkbases. Linkbases can point to schemata or to other linkbases.

```
<xbrli:xbrl
      xmlns:xbrli="http://www.xbrl.org/2003/instance"
      xmlns:link="http://www.xbrl.org/2003/linkbase"
      xmlns:xlink="http://www.w3.org/1999/xlink">

  <link:linkbaseRef
      xlink:href="taxonomy-lab.xml"
      xlink:role=
        "http://www.xbrl.org/2003/role/labelLinkbaseRef"
      xlink:arcrole=
        "http://www.w3.org/1999/xlink/properties/linkbase"
      xlink:type="simple" />

  <!-- other linkbaseRefs, schemaRefs -->
  <!-- contexts, units and facts -->

</xbrli:xbrl>
```

Figure 4.13: A simple link to a hypothetical taxonomy linkbase named taxonomy-lab.xml and located in the same directory, in an instance.

4.6.9   Linking from a linkbase

Linkbases can also link to further schemata and linkbases, contributing them to the DTS.

To a schema

Any locator used to point to a concept has an `xlink:href` attribute pointing to a taxonomy schema. This taxonomy schema is then included in the DTS.

To a linkbase

A locator can, in certain cases not covered yet, point to an XML fragment in a linkbase rather than in a schema. In such cases, the

```
<xs:schema
    xmlns:xs="http://www.w3.org/2001/XMLSchema"
    xmlns:link="http://www.xbrl.org/2003/linkbase"
    xmlns:xlink="http://www.w3.org/1999/xlink"
    targetNamespace="http://example.com/my-namespace">

  <xs:annotation>

    <xs:appinfo>

      <link:linkbaseRef
        xlink:href="http://www.example.com/taxonomy-lab.xml"
        xlink:role=
          "http://www.xbrl.org/2003/role/labelLinkbaseRef"
        xlink:arcrole=
          "http://www.w3.org/1999/xlink/properties/linkbase"
        xlink:type="simple" />

      <!-- further references to linkbases and schemata -->

    </xs:appinfo>

  </xs:annotation>

  <!-- element and type definitions -->

</xs:schema>
```

Figure 4.14: A simple link to a taxonomy linkbase located on the Web, in a taxonomy schema.

referenced linkbase is included into the DTS as well.

We will see in Chapter 5 that further references (role references, arc role references) made in a linkbase can add further linkbases to the DTS.

4.6.10   Nesting a linkbase in a taxonomy schema

It is also possible, yet not recommended, to directly put extended links such as `link:labelLink` inside the `xs:appinfo` element en-

```
<xs:schema
    xmlns:xs="http://www.w3.org/2001/XMLSchema"
    xmlns:link="http://www.xbrl.org/2003/linkbase"
    xmlns:xlink="http://www.w3.org/1999/xlink"
    targetNamespace="http://example.com/my-namespace">

  <xs:annotation>

    <xs:appinfo>

      <link:labelLink
          xlink:role="http://www.xbrl.org/2003/role/link"
          xlink:type="extended">
        <!-- nodes and edges -->
      <link:labelLink/>
        <!-- further extended links or references to
            schemata and linkbases -->

    </xs:appinfo>

  </xs:annotation>

  <!-- element and type definitions -->

</xs:schema>
```

Figure 4.15: A linkbase as an extended link nested inside a schema.

countered earlier. This is shown on Figure 4.15.

Chapter 5

Presentation

In Chapter 2, we introduced facts and showed how they can be presented in highly structured fact tables. We then introduced concepts (Chapter 3), which describe *what* a fact is about, and showed how these concepts can be associated with human-friendly labels (Chapter 4).

We now have all the pieces in place to introduce the XBRL machinery for presenting facts in a nice way, or to be fair to fact tables, in a way that is more usual for accountants than fact tables: have you ever seen a fiscal report presented as a flat list of facts?

Through this chapter and later, we will use as examples the sample instances and taxonomies from a Sample Company, provided by Charles Hoffman, available at `http://www.xbrlsite.c om/DigitalFinancialReporting/Metapatterns/2013-05-15/`. These are a very good starting point to understand presentation and best practices.

5.1   Individual facts

Facts can be displayed one at a time. This typically happens when the business user, working on a report, needs to look into the details of a single fact, for example by clicking on a value in a user-friendly document that has its values tagged with an XBRL context[1], or by clicking on a row in a fact table, a cell in a spreadsheet, etc.

The most low-level way to display a single fact, other than the raw XML syntax of course, is shown on Figure 5.1a. It uses:

- the internal SQNames for the concepts and units

- as well as an SQName according to the Open Information Model for the entity, using a custom prefix in lieu of the entity scheme

- the lexical dates for periods, with durations represented with slashes such as 2015-12-01/2015-12-31.

- SQNames for standard aspects, with the oim, provided by the Open Information Model. The latter do not appear in the XBRL syntax and are only here for data modeling purposes.

As you can see, there is nothing left of XML at this first level of abstraction.

Figure 5.1 also shows this same fact with English labels and hypothetical French labels. The labels for the concepts come from the label linkbase, as introduced in Chapter 4. The other labels, be it for standard aspects[2], for formatting dates and units, or for figuring out a user-friendly name for an entity, are left to the XBRL user-facing UI and do not appear in any taxonomy. The entity

---

[1]We refer to iXBRL, which inlines XBRL facts in HTML documents.

[2]We will see, when we introduce user-defined aspects in a subsequent edition (with XBRL dimensions), that their labels as well as the labels of the associated aspect values will also be defined with label linkbases in taxonomies.

Aspect	Characteristic
oim:concept	pattern:BuildingNet
oim:entity	samp:SAMP
oim:period	2010-12-31
oim:unit	iso4217:USD
Fact value	5,347,000

(a) A numeric fact, shown with no labels. We use the Open Information Model SQNames for standard aspects.

Aspect	Characteristic
Concept	Buildings, Net
Entity	Sample Company
Period	December 31, 2010
Unit	U.S. Dollars
Fact value	5,347,000

(b) A numeric fact, shown with labels.

Aspect	Charactéristique
Concept	Immeubles, Net
Entité	Sample Company
Période	31 décembre 2010
Unité	Dollars américains
Valeur	5,347,000 ˙

(c) A numeric fact, shown with labels in French.

Figure 5.1: A numeric fact, shown in different ways.

name, though, may be smartly extracted from an instance. For example, in EDGAR filings, there is always a fact reported against the concept `dei:EntityRegistrantName` that can be used as a label for the reporting entity.

5.2 Fact tables

Often, facts are not displayed one at a time, but in meaningful groups: for example, a balance sheet or an income statement. Figures 5.2 and 5.3 show a table with 8 facts all containing text about the accounting policies of our sample company, each of them shown in a row. As in the previous section, we show it once using the internal names (5.2), and once using the labels from the label linkbase (5.3).

Figure 5.4 shows another example with numeric values reporting the property, plant and equipment of our sample company.

As for individual facts, nothing is left from the original XML syntax, and a business user can understand the data shown as fact tables with no IT knowledge. Furthermore, fact tables as shown on Figures 5.2, 5.3 or 5.4 can be saved as csv (comma-separated values) files and be imported in Excel or any other spreadsheet software in a straightforward way. With Excel's pivot table feature, one can then slice and dice the data conveniently.

Hence, fact tables are the representation of choice that is both user-friendly, in that no knowledge of the XBRL syntax is required to understand it, but it is also still machine-readable since spreadsheet software can do very useful things including analysis, aggregation and all kinds of charts with it.

5.3 Networks

In our two former examples of fact tables, the facts were grouped in a meaningful way: numeric facts describing property, plant and

oim:concept	oim:entity	oim:period	value
pattern:BasisOfPresentation	samp:SAMP	2010-01-01/2010-12-31	Praesent fringilla feugiat magna. Suspendisse et lorem eu risus convallis placerat.Suspendisse potenti. Donec malesuada loremid mi. Nunc ut purus ac nisl tempus accumsan.
pattern:InventoryValuationMethod	samp:SAMP	2010-01-01/2010-12-31	Cost.
pattern:DescriptionOfInventoryComponents	samp:SAMP	2010-01-01/2010-12-31	Proin elit sem, ornare non, ullamcorper vel, sollicitudin a, lacus. Mauris tincidunt cursus est. Nulla sit amet nibh. Sed elementum feugiat augue. Nam non tortor non leo porta bibendum. Morbi eu pede.
pattern:InventoryCostMethod	samp:SAMP	2010-01-01/2010-12-31	FIFO
pattern:TradeReceivablesPolicy	samp:SAMP	2010-01-01/2010-12-31	Sed magna felis, accumsan a, fermentum quis, varius sed, ipsum. Nullam leo. Donec eros.
pattern:InvestmentsInSecuritiesPolicy	samp:SAMP	2010-01-01/2010-12-31	Etiam ipsum orci, gravida nec, feugiat ut, malesuada quis, mauris. Etiam porttitor. Ut venenatis, velit a accumsan interdum, odio metus mollis mauris, non pharetra augue arcu eu felis.
pattern:BankBorrowingsPolicy	samp:SAMP	2010-01-01/2010-12-31	Ut ut risus nec nibh dictum posuere. Phasellus eleifend, diam vitae dapibus pulvinar, erat ligula auctor dui, eget conguejusto lorem hendrerit tellus.
pattern:ProvisionsPolicySuspendisse	samp:SAMP	2010-01-01/2010-12-31	vestibulum augue eu justo. Pellentesque habitant morbi tristique senectus et netus et malesuada fames ac turpis egestas.

Figure 5.2: A fact table containing text blocks, shown without and with labels. The facts describe the accounting policy of our sample company. With raw names.

Concept	Entity	Period	Value
Basis Of Presentation	Sample Company	Jan. 1 to Dec. 31st, 2010	Praesent fringilla feugiat magna. Suspendisse et lorem eu risus convallis placerat.Suspendisse potenti. Donec malesuada loremid mi. Nunc ut purus ac nisl tempus accumsan.
Inventory Valuation Method	Sample Company	Jan. 1 to Dec. 31st, 2010	Cost
Description Of Inventory Components	Sample Company	Jan. 1 to Dec. 31st, 2010	Proin elit sem, ornare non, ullamcorper vel, sollicitudin a, lacus. Mauris tincidunt cursus est. Nulla sit amet nibh. Sed elementum feugiat augue. Nam non tortor non leo porta bibendum. Morbi eu pede.
Inventory Cost Method	Sample Company	Jan. 1 to Dec. 31st, 2010	FIFO
Trade Receivables Policy	Sample Company	Jan. 1 to Dec. 31st, 2010	Sed magna felis, accumsan a, fermentum quis, varius sed, ipsum. Nullam leo. Donec eros.
Investments In Securities Policy	Sample Company	Jan. 1 to Dec. 31st, 2010	Etiam ipsum orci, gravida nec, feugiat ut, malesuada quis, mauris. Etiam porttitor. Ut venenatis, velit a accumsan interdum, odio metus mollis mauris, non pharetra augue arcu eu felis.
Bank Borrowings Policy	Sample Company	Jan. 1 to Dec. 31st, 2010	Ut ut risus nec nibh dictum posuere. Phasellus eleifend, diam vitae dapibus pulvinar, erat ligula auctor dui, eget conguejusto lorem hendrerit tellus.
Provisions Policy Suspendisse	Sample Company	Jan. 1 to Dec. 31st, 2010	vestibulum augue eu justo. Pellentesque habitant morbi tristique senectus et netus et malesuada fames ac turpis egestas.

Figure 5.3: A fact table containing text blocks, shown without and with labels. The facts describe the accounting policy of our sample company. With labels (standard label roles in English are used).

oim:concept	oim:entity	oim:period	oim:unit	value
pattern:Land	samp:SAMP	2010-12-31	iso4217:USD	5347000
pattern:Land	samp:SAMP	2009-12-31	iso4217:USD	1147000
pattern:BuildingsNet	samp:SAMP	2010-12-31	iso4217:USD	244508000
pattern:BuildingsNet	samp:SAMP	2009-12-31	iso4217:USD	366375000
pattern:FurnitureAndFixturesNet	samp:SAMP	2010-12-31	iso4217:USD	34457000
pattern:FurnitureAndFixturesNet	samp:SAMP	2009-12-31	iso4217:USD	34457000
pattern:ComputerEquipmentNet	samp:SAMP	2010-12-31	iso4217:USD	4169000
pattern:ComputerEquipmentNet	samp:SAMP	2009-12-31	iso4217:USD	5313000
pattern:OtherPropertyPlantAndEquipmentNet	samp:SAMP	2010-12-31	iso4217:USD	6702000
pattern:OtherPropertyPlantAndEquipmentNet	samp:SAMP	2009-12-31	iso4217:USD	6149000
pattern:PropertyPlantAndEquipmentNet	samp:SAMP	2010-12-31	iso4217:USD	295183000
pattern:PropertyPlantAndEquipmentNet	samp:SAMP	2009-12-31	iso4217:USD	413441000

(a) With raw names.

Concept	Entity	Period	Unit	Value
Land	Sample Company	Dec 31, 2010	US Dollars	5,347,000
Land	Sample Company	Dec 31, 2009	US Dollars	1,147,000
Buildings, Net	Sample Company	Dec 31, 2010	US Dollars	244,508,000
Buildings, Net	Sample Company	Dec 31, 2009	US Dollars	366,375,000
Furniture And Fixtures, Net	Sample Company	Dec 31, 2010	US Dollars	34,457,000
Furniture And Fixtures, Net	Sample Company	Dec 31, 2009	US Dollars	34,457,000
Computer Equipment, Net	Sample Company	Dec 31, 2010	US Dollars	4,169,000
Computer Equipment, Net	Sample Company	Dec 31, 2009	US Dollars	5,313,000
Other Property, Plant and Equipment, Net	Sample Company	Dec 31, 2010	US Dollars	6,702,000
Other Property, Plant and Equipment, Net	Sample Company	Dec 31, 2009	US Dollars	6,149,000
Property, Plant and Equipment, Net	Sample Company	Dec 31, 2010	US Dollars	295,183,000
Property, Plant and Equipment, Net	Sample Company	Dec 31, 2009	US Dollars	413,441,000

(b) With standard labels in English.

Figure 5.4: A fact table showing numeric facts representing the property, plant and equipment of our sample company, without and with labels.

equipment on one side, and textual facts describing accounting policies on the other side. Of course, it would still be possible to create a single fact table with all these facts. It may not look very good because there is some heterogeneity in these facts: textual facts have no unit for example. But it would work.

However: who writes a book with a single chapter, or a fiscal report with just one single section? It is very natural to organize reports in sections. In XBRL, a section in a report is called a network[3], for reasons that will soon become apparent.

5.3.1 Network identifiers

A network can be internally identified with a URI[4].

In our former example, the URI of the accounting policy network is `http://www.xbrlsite.com/DigitalFinancialReporting` `/Metapattern/Hierarchy/AccountingPolicies` and that of the plant, property of equipment network is `http://www.xbrlsite.c` `om/DigitalFinancialReporting/Metapattern/RollUp/Property` `PlantAndEquipmentByComponent`.

Even though it is confusing that network identifiers, that is, URIs[5], like namespace URIs, often begin with the HTTP scheme, these are not URLs[6] and, as such, they most likely will not work if you try them in a browser.

5.3.2 Network labels

For user-friendliness, networks also have labels that can be understood by humans, so that network identifiers do not need to actually be shown to the end user – just as you wouldn't show

---

[3]We follow the terminology suggested by Charles Hoffman

[4]For XBRL-savvy people, this corresponds to a link role in the underlying syntax

[5]Universal Resource Identifier

[6]Universal Resource Locator

URIs in the fancy printed version of a fiscal report. The network labels corresponding to our two example sections are:

20000 - Accounting Policies

30000 - Property, Plant, and Equipment, by Component

It is not uncommon, although not required, to including a numbering scheme in the network labels for organizing and ordering networks. EDGAR filings typically use such a scheme. XBRL, however, is not aware of such a scheme and just considers the entire string to be the label.

Unlike concept labels, multiple languages are not supported on network labels. English is typically used for multilingual reports.

5.4 Model structures

5.4.1 Presentation networks

So we have seen that facts are grouped in networks – more precisely, we would say that networks are used to group facts. How are facts grouped in networks, and how are they organized in a network?

The first thing to know is that networks are not built by simply throwing facts into a bag: it would be more accurate to say that they are built by throwing *concepts* into a bag, and all the facts in an instance that have this concept then belong to the network. All these facts can thus be presented as a fact table as shown in Section 5.2. Each concept can appear in multiple networks.

The second thing to know is that networks are not made of a single, flat list of concepts. In fact, within a network, concepts are organized in trees known as presentation networks[7]. If you think of a balance sheet or an income statement for a second, you will find it obvious that there is some structure involved: for example, there are assets on one side, and liabilities and equity on the other side, etc.

---

[7]Charles Hoffman uses the term model structure.

http://www.xbrlsite.com/DigitalFinancialReporting/Metapattern/ Hierarchy/AccountingPolicies
pattern:AccountingPoliciesAbstract
pattern:BasisOfPresentation
pattern:TradeReceivablesPolicy
pattern:InventoryPoliciesAbstract
pattern:InventoryValuationMethod
pattern:DescriptionOfInventoryComponents
pattern:InventoryCostMethod
pattern:InvestmentsInSecuritiesPolicy
pattern:BankBorrowingsPolicy
pattern:ProvisionsPolicy

(a) The presentation network for our sample company's accounting policies.

http://www.xbrlsite.com/DigitalFinancialReporting/Metapattern/ RollUp/PropertyPlantAndEquipmentByComponent
pattern:PropertyPlantAndEquipmentNetAbstract
pattern:Land
pattern:BuildingsNet
pattern:FurnitureAndFixturesNet
pattern:ComputerEquipmentNet
pattern:OtherPropertyPlantAndEquipmentNet
pattern:PropertyPlantAndEquipmentNet

(b) The presentation network for our sample company's net property, plant and equipment.

Figure 5.5: Two presentation networks

Figure 5.5 shows the presentation networks associated with our two fact tables shown on Figure 5.2 and Figure 5.4.

5.4.2 Presentation linkbases

The union of all presentation networks, that is, across networks, is called the presentation linkbase.

We already saw a kind of linkbase in Chapter 4: label linkbases. Presentation linkbases are another kind of linkbase and, like label linkbases, they are graphs. However, while label linkbases are bipartite graphs of concepts and labels, presentation linkbases are trees or DAGs of concepts, as shown on Figure 5.6. The two examples shown on Figure 5.5 are trees.

An aspect that may cause confusion is how linkbases and networks relate. We give an approach that should help clarifying things, but with the warning that not everybody in the XBRL community may agree on the exact granularity of networks or linkbases[8].

Linkbases and networks can be seen as two ways of segmenting the "big graph", that is, the graph containing all nodes and edges defined in a taxonomy linkbase, no matter what their semantics is. A bit like a music sheet can be either segmented by movements, or by instruments.

The big graph can be segmented into networks, which correspond to semantic units exposed to the user (for example: a balance sheet, an income statement, a cash flow statement, etc). Networks

---

[8]We use the term "network" as suggested by Charles Hoffman, that is, as a synonym for link role. The specification, in fact, defines a network as the set of edges with the same link role, link name, arc role and arc name, but we prefer to stay away from this definition because it is very low-level and not suitable for learning XBRL on the level of its data model. The reason why the level of granularity is not clear is simple: a network is a graph, and, from a mathematical perspective, any sub-graph of a graph is itself a graph as well. Hence, it is a matter of agreeing on, and sticking to a convention regarding the granularity.

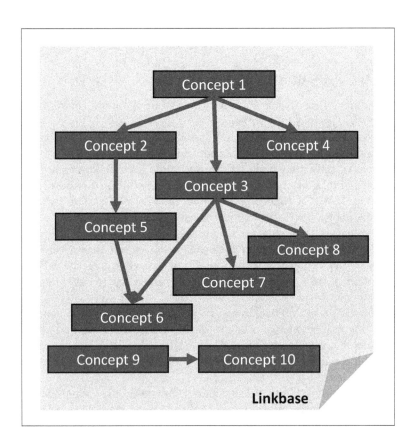

Figure 5.6: A presentation linkbase, which is a directed acyclic graph. Each edge connects a concept with another concept. Directed cycles are not allowed, but undirected cycles are allowed (one is shown with two arrows pointing to Concept 6). In this case, the presentation linkbase consists of two presentation networks, but in general there will be several of them.

are a bit like vertical slices of the graph, like movements in a music sheet, but across all instruments.

The big graph can also, instead, be segmented into linkbases, which correspond to logical units that are not exposed to the user directly and that play different roles in XBRL: a label linkbase to associate concepts with labels, a presentation linkbase to organize concepts in hierarchies, and we will see more linkbases in upcoming chapters, such as the calculation linkbase. Linkbases are a bit like horizontal slices of the graph, acting a bit like various instruments on a music sheet, but across all movements.

It is also possible to identify a sub-graph by selecting the intersection of a network and a linkbase from the big graph, in which case we call it a presentation network, a label network, etc. This corresponds to a single instrument in a single movement in our sheet music analogy. If a report contains, say, 5 networks and 2 linkbases, this gives us in theory 10 of these more specific networks.

It should be noted that label linkbases are very often not organized across networks. Instead, all labels are associated with concepts in the same network, the default network, as shown in Chapter 4. When presenting each network to the user, labels will hence be taken from the default label network. However, each network can still contain a label network in order to override some labels (not necessarily all the ones it uses) within its scope. This is commonly done as well.

5.4.3 Ordering of edges and display

The order in which concepts appear in a presentation linkbase is important: the children of each node in the tree or DAG are ordered. In other words, edges in a presentation linkbase are annotated not only with the network identifier, but also with a number that indicates its order among the edges that originate from the same parent within a network.

Often, presentation linkbases are displayed not as an explicit graph, but as a list of concepts that are ordered and indented according to the way they nest. This is as shown on Figure 5.5. This is straightforward if the presentation linkbase is a tree. If, however, it is a DAG, it can then be expanded to a tree by duplicated nodes met in cycles, which allows a user-friendly display as well.

5.5   Abstracts

5.5.1   A new kind of report element

If you look closer and compare the fact tables shown on Figure 5.2 and Figure 5.4 to the presentation networks represented on Figure 5.5, you will notice that there are three "concepts"[9] that do not appear anywhere in the fact table, because no facts are reported against them:

- `pattern:AccountingPoliciesAbstract`,

- `pattern:InventoryPoliciesAbstract`,

- `pattern:PropertyPlantAndEquipmentNetAbstract`

These items are in fact not concepts[10]: they are abstracts. And both concepts and abstracts belong to a broader category called report elements[11]. We will later see more kinds of report elements, but for now we only have abstracts and concepts.

---

[9]The word is quoted because, as we will see shortly, these are not concepts in the sense that they were introduced in Chapter 3.

[10]In the XBRL specification, they would be referred to as abstract concepts. However, as we previously said, we only use the word concept for non-abstract concepts.

[11]In XBRL specifications, report elements would be called items, and abstracts would be called abstract primary items

All report elements, that is, not only concepts, appear in the taxonomy schemata introduced in Chapter 3. This means that the taxonomy schema is a flat list of report elements, among which concepts, abstracts, etc.

Likewise, any report elements can appear in a linkbase. This means that they can appear in a presentation linkbase as shown on Figure 5.5, but also in a label linkbase. Hence, more generally, linkbases are graphs involving report elements (like concepts and abstracts) and resources (like labels).

Abstracts are simply here to give some structure to the presentation linkbase: the top-level abstracts, `pattern:Accounting\pro` `tect\discretionary{\char\hyphenchar\font}{}{}PoliciesAbs` `tract` and `pattern:PropertyPlantAndEquipmentNetAbstract`, wrap up the entire hierarchy, while the other one, `pattern:Inventor` `yPoliciesAbstract`, groups a smaller set of concepts as a sub-hierarchy. Often, abstracts will be used as non-leaves in the tree, and concepts as leaves.

If you now take a closer look, you will notice that the qualified names of the abstracts end with `Abstract`.

It is very common practice, although not required by XBRL, to stamp report elements other than concepts with such suffixes. It makes presentation networks, but also renderings as we will see later, easier to understand. Some regulatory authorities such as the SEC make use of these stamps mandatory, and it is important to note that the stamps and their usage will vary from authority to authority, as it is outside of the scope of XBRL itself.

5.5.2   Abstract metadata

We have now encountered two kinds of report elements: concepts and abstracts.

From a data model perspective, unlike concepts, abstracts do

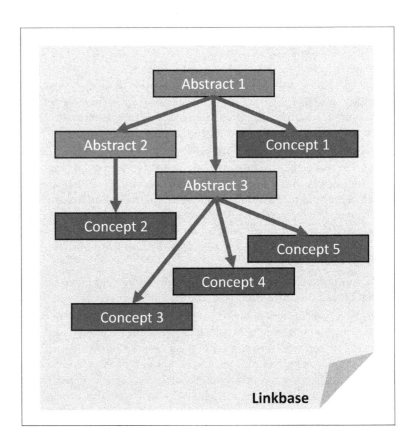

Figure 5.7: A presentation linkbase involving abstracts for non-leaves. This one consists of only one presentation network with no undirected cycles.

not have any metadata apart from the fact they are abstracts[12]. Abstracts do not have a data type, period or balance, simply because no facts are reported against them. Figure 5.8 shows the presentation linkbase including the metadata for each report element.

5.5.3 Abstract labels

Abstracts, and more generally any report elements, can also be associated to labels, and this is done in exactly the same way as concepts, that is, as a bipartite graph with report elements and labels. The only exception is that some label roles (such as total labels, negative labels, and so on) do not make any sense for report elements other than concepts, so that the standard label role will typically be used for them.

5.6 Selecting labels

We saw in Chapter 4 that concepts can be associated with multiple labels, and in Section 5.5 that this machinery is also extended to abstracts. Each label has a label role and a language that allows to identify it.

5.6.1 Preferred label roles

It is possible, for each report element in a model structure, to specify which label role should be used for display. This mechanism is called preferred label role.

Each edge in the presentation linkbase is annotated with a preferred label role, as shown on Figure 5.9. This preferred label role

---

[12]However, when we tackle the XBRL syntax for presentation networks, we will see that abstracts actually do have data types and period types on a syntactic level. However, this is irrelevant from a data model perspective, and many regulatory authorities such as the SEC require standard values for these.

http://www.xbrlsite.com/DigitalFinancialReporting/Metapattern/Hierarchy/AccountingPolicies

Report element	Kind	Type	Period Type
pattern:AccountingPoliciesHierarchy	Abstract	-	-
pattern:BasisOfPresentation	Concept	nonnum:textBlockItemType	instant
pattern:TradeReceivablesPolicy	Concept	nonnum:textBlockItemType	instant
pattern:InventoryPoliciesAbstract	Abstract	-	-
pattern:InventoryValuationMethod	Concept	nonnum:textBlockItemType	instant
pattern:DescriptionOfInventoryComponents	Concept	nonnum:textBlockItemType	instant
pattern:InventoryCostMethod	Concept	nonnum:textBlockItemType	instant
pattern:InvestmentsInSecuritiesPolicy	Concept	nonnum:textBlockItemType	instant
pattern:BankBorrowingsPolicy	Concept	nonnum:textBlockItemType	instant
pattern:ProvisionsPolicy	Concept	nonnum:textBlockItemType	instant

(a) Presentation network for accounting policies with metadata. Balance is omitted as there are no concepts with a monetary data type.

http://www.xbrlsite.com/DigitalFinancialReporting/Metapattern/RollUp/PropertyPlantAndEquipmentByComponent

Report element	Kind	Type	Balance	Period Type
pattern:PropertyPlantAndEquipmentNetRollUp	Abstract	-	-	-
pattern:Land	Concept	xbrli:monetaryItemType	debit	instant
pattern:BuildingsNet	Concept	xbrli:monetaryItemType	debit	instant
pattern:FurnitureAndFixturesNet	Concept	xbrli:monetaryItemType	debit	instant
pattern:ComputerEquipmentNet	Concept	xbrli:monetaryItemType	debit	instant
pattern:OtherPropertyPlantAndEquipmentNet	Concept	xbrli:monetaryItemType	debit	instant
pattern:PropertyPlantAndEquipmentNet	Concept	xbrli:monetaryItemType	debit	instant

(b) Presentation network for property, plant and equipment with metadata.

Figure 5.8: The presentation linkbase for our sample company's accounting policies, including report element metadata.

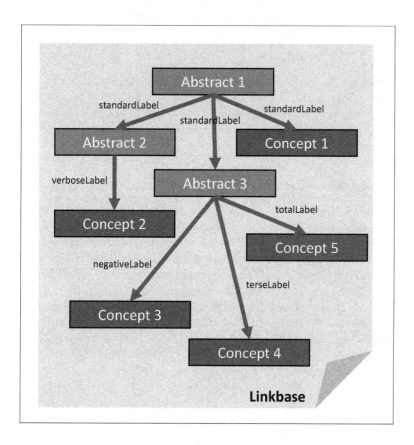

Figure 5.9: A hypothetical presentation linkbase with preferred label roles on edges. Only the last parts of the label role URIs are shown.

is a URI that corresponds to the label role of one of the labels associated with the report element in the label linkbase.

5.6.2 Languages

Selecting the language is left to the UI, which may or may not provide a user with a choice of the language to display. In practice, instances and taxonomies very often contain either a single language, or a single language and English, or more languages if the usage spans over a geographical area involving many languages.

5.6.3 Showing the presentation linkbase with labels

Figure 5.10 shows our two presentation linkbases as textual trees, but now using labels. For simplicity, we are assuming that all preferred label roles are set to the standard label role. We will see examples of presentation with different preferred label roles (total, periodStart, periodEnd) in later chapters.

The figure also shows the metadata, to illustrate that it can also be displayed in a user-friendly way: the UI can display user-friendly labels for types as well. Since XBRL does not support type labels per se, however, it is on the UI implementer to take care of this. Since most types are standardized XBRL types, whether core or from a registry, it can be done with a simple map.

5.7 Presenting facts

Now that we introduced networks and showed how report elements in a network are arranged in hierarchies known as presentation networks, we have everything we need to fancily display all facts of a network.

The renderings shown on Figures 5.11 and 5.12 correspond to the vision of Charles Hoffman, and this is implemented by several

20000 - Accounting Policies

Report element	Kind	Type	Period Type
Accounting policies [Abstract]	Abstract	-	-
Basis of presentation	Concept	Text block	instant
Trade receivables policy	Concept	Text block	instant
Inventory policies [Abstract]	Abstract	-	-
Inventory valuation method	Concept	Text block	instant
Description of inventory components	Concept	Text block	instant
Inventory cost method	Concept	Text block	instant
Investments in securities policy	Concept	Text block	instant
Bank borrowing policy	Concept	Text block	instant
Provisions policy	Concept	Text block	instant

(a) The accounting policies, shown with labels according to the roles selected in the presentation linkbase.

30000 - Property, Plant, and Equipment, by Component

Report element	Kind	Type	Balance	Period Type
Property, plant and equipment [Abstract]	Abstract	-	-	-
Land	Concept	Monetary	debit	instant
Buildings, net	Concept	Monetary	debit	instant
Furniture and fixtures, net	Concept	Monetary	debit	instant
Computer equipment, net	Concept	Monetary	debit	instant
Other property, plant and equipment, net	Concept	Monetary	debit	instant
Property, plant and equipment, net	Concept	Monetary	debit	instant

(b) The Property, plant and equipment, shown with labels according to the roles selected in the presentation linkbase.

Figure 5.10: The presentation linkbases, displayed in a user-friendly fashion using labels

vendors. The main idea is that the facts populating each network[13] form a data cube – in this case, both have four dimensions (one for each aspect) – and this data cube must be flattened to two dimensions to fit on paper. This is done by assigning each aspect to either be a slicer, or to be a dicer on a row or column. Very commonly, concepts are on rows, and other aspects (period, entity, etc) are on columns, or are slicers if they only have one value. A few UIs, today, already allow interactive slicing and dicing of single sections, in a way very similar to Excel's pivot table feature.

The first rendering, on Figure 5.11 has four aspects: concept, entity, period, language. Everywhere in the renderings, aspect names appear in a dark blue background, often stamped with [Axis], whereas aspect values appear in a light blue background. The period, entity and language aspects, which share the same value for all facts, are set up as slicers at the top. The concept aspect is assigned to rows. The latter is a bit special, because, in lieu of the concept aspect name (which could have been "Concept [Axis]"), the top-level abstract of the presentation network is promoted to the dark blue main header.

The first rendering, on Figure 5.11 has four aspects: concept, entity, period, unit. The entity and unit aspects, which share the same value for all facts, are set up as slicers at the top. The concept aspect is assigned to rows and the period aspect, with two values, is assigned to columns.

5.8   Concept arrangement patterns

Presentation linkbases, from an XBRL perspective, can be any DAGs of report elements. However, there are some common practices or best practices that emerged in the past few years. Some of

---

[13]For pedagogical purposes. Actually, when hypercubes (XBRL dimensions) are in the game, networks can contain several components, each of which is a data cube.

Network	20000 - Accounting Policies
Entity [Axis]	Sample Company
Period [Axis]	Jan. 1 to Dec. 31st, 2010
Language [Axis]	U.S. English
Accounting policies [Abstract]	
Basis of presentation	Praesent fringilla feugiat magna. Suspendisse et lorem eu risus convallis placerat.Suspendisse potenti. Donec malesuada loremid mi. Nunc ut purus ac nisl tempus accumsan.
Trade receivables policy	Sed magna felis, accumsan a, fermentum quis, varius sed, ipsum. Nullam leo. Donec eros.
Inventory policies [Abstract]	
Inventory valuation method	Cost
Description of inventory components	Proin elit sem, ornare non, ullamcorper vel, sollicitudin a, lacus. Mauris tincidunt cursus est. Nulla sit amet nibh. Sed elementum feugiat augue. Nam
Inventory cost method	FIFO
Investments in securities policy	Etiam ipsum orci, gravida nec, feugiat ut, malesuada quis, mauris. Etiam porttitor. Ut venenatis, velit a accumsan interdum, odio metus mollis mauris, non pharetra augue arcu eu felis.
Bank borrowing policy	Ut ut risus nec nibh dictum posuere. Phasellus eleifend, diam vitae dapibus pulvinar, erat ligula auctor dui, eget conguejusto lorem hendrerit tellus.
Provisions policy	vestibulum augue eu justo. Pellentesque habitant morbi tristique senectus et netus et malesuada fames ac turpis egestas.

Figure 5.11: The accounting policies network, in a user-friendly fashion using labels.

Network	30000 - Property, Plant, and Equipment, by Component

Entity [Axis]	Sample Company
Unit [Axis]	U.S. Dollars

Property, plant and equipment [Abstract]	Period [Axis]	
	Jan. 1 to Dec. 31st, 2009	Jan. 1 to Dec. 31st, 2010
Land	1,147,000	5,347,000
Buildings, net	366,375,000	244,508,000
Furniture and fixtures, net	34,457,000	34,457,000
Computer equipment, net	5,313,000	4,169,000
Other property, plant and equipment, net	6,149,000	6,702,000
Property, plant and equipment, net	413,441,000	295,183,000

Figure 5.12: The Property, plant and equipment network, in a user-friendly fashion using labels.

these practices are enforced by regulatory authorities such as the SEC, while some other are more something that companies tend to do. Hence, many fiscal reports filed to the SEC share similar patterns in their presentation linkbases. Charles Hoffman identified and categorized the most common structures, and recommends to stick to them to the extent possible.

These patterns are not standardized by the XBRL consortium and have no binding value except when regulatory authorities decide to. Some regulatory authorities using the DPM have completely different conventions and, as explained earlier, rely on table linkbases rather than presentation linkbases for rendering the facts. For the moment, we leave aside reporting based on table linkbases and focus on reporting based on what we could call network partitioning, i.e., where the data is organized and partitioned in presentation networks.

Abstract	Abstract
Abstract	Abstract
Concept	Concept
Concept	Concept
Abstract	Concept
Concept	Concept
Abstract	Abstract
Concept	Concept
Concept	Concept
(a) Recommended: only abstracts have children.	(b) Done in practice, but not advised

Figure 5.13: Examples of how presentation networks organize report elements in a hierarchy.

5.8.1 Abstracts in presentation networks

Each presentation network is commonly organized as a single hierarchy with the top-level report element being an abstract as shown on Figure 5.13. Each abstract may contain concepts, but also further abstracts. Concepts are most of the time leaves in the hierarchy, even though it does happen in practice that some companies nest concepts or even sometimes abstracts below concepts. We do not recommend doing so.

For pedagogical purposes, we leave out other kinds of report elements at that point.

Both networks shown before (i.e., rendered on Figures 5.11 and 5.12) strictly adhere to these guidelines. Further guidelines organize presentation networks according to diverse patterns, but these general guidelines apply to all of them.

In EDGAR filings, most abstracts are simply stamped with their names ending in `Abstract`. Some abstracts may, instead, contain some more specific stamps such as `Hierarchy` or `RollUp`.

These stamps typically appear on labels in square brackets as well: [Abstract], [Hierarchy], [RollUp].

5.8.2   Three concept arrangement patterns

Figures 5.14 and 5.15 show a slightly different version of our two renderings linkbases, where the top-level abstract names have been changed to explicitly refer to the presentation networks as a hierarchy and as a roll-up pattern[14].

These two patterns are two examples of ways that presentation networks are typically organized in practice: hierarchy and roll-up. There are of course more of them, but these two are a good way to start with presentation networks.

Within a presentation linkbase, each presentation network may use a different pattern, that is, hierarchies, roll-ups and others can cohabit.

We now present three patterns more in details. These are the patterns that do not involve dimensions and thus only use the material introduced until now.

Hierarchy pattern

Hierarchies, such as the accounting policies example, would correspond to the most general pattern for a presentation network and typically is the only one that makes sense with non-numeric facts. A hierarchy should have a top-level abstract (the one stamped as Hierarchy), as well as any tree of concepts and abstracts below this top-level abstract. If possible, one should only nest report elements below abstracts, as previously explained. Hierarchies typically have non-numeric facts such as text blocks.

---

[14]The top-level abstracts are still categorized as abstract, even though their name is suffixed with Hierarchy or RollUp. Hierarchies are a pattern, but not a kind of report element

Network	20000 - Accounting Policies
Entity [Axis]	Sample Company
Period [Axis]	Jan. 1 to Dec. 31st, 2010
Language [Axis]	U.S. English

Accounting policies [Hierarchy]	
Basis of presentation	Praesent fringilla feugiat magna. Suspendisse et lorem eu risus convallis placerat.Suspendisse potenti. Donec malesuada loremid mi. Nunc ut purus ac nisl tempus accumsan.
Trade receivables policy	Sed magna felis, accumsan a, fermentum quis, varius sed, ipsum. Nullam leo. Donec eros.
Inventory policies [Abstract]	
Inventory valuation method	Cost
Description of inventory components	Proin elit sem, ornare non, ullamcorper vel, sollicitudin a, lacus. Mauris tincidunt cursus est. Nulla sit amet nibh. Sed elementum feugiat augue. Nam
Inventory cost method	FIFO
Investments in securities policy	Etiam ipsum orci, gravida nec, feugiat ut, malesuada quis, mauris. Etiam porttitor. Ut venenatis, velit a accumsan interdum, odio metus mollis mauris, non pharetra augue arcu eu felis.
Bank borrowing policy	Ut ut risus nec nibh dictum posuere. Phasellus eleifend, diam vitae dapibus pulvinar, erat ligula auctor dui, eget conguejusto lorem hendrerit tellus.
Provisions policy	vestibulum augue eu justo. Pellentesque habitant morbi tristique senectus et netus et malesuada fames ac turpis egestas.

Figure 5.14: The accounting policies network, presented as a hierarchy pattern.

Network	30000 - Property, Plant, and Equipment, by Component
Entity [Axis]	Sample Company
Unit [Axis]	U.S. Dollars

Property, plant and equipment [RollUp]	Period [Axis]	
	Jan. 1 to Dec. 31st, 2009	Jan. 1 to Dec. 31st, 2010
Land	1,147,000	5,347,000
Buildings, net	366,375,000	244,508,000
Furniture and fixtures, net	34,457,000	34,457,000
Computer equipment, net	5,313,000	4,169,000
Other property, plant and equipment, net	6,149,000	6,702,000
Property, plant and equipment, net , total	413,441,000	295,183,000

Figure 5.15: The Property, plant and equipment network, presented with a roll up pattern (with a preferred total label role on the last row).

Roll-up pattern

Roll-ups, such as in the property, plant and equipment example, will be studied more in details in Chapter 6, as they involve more computing machinery. However, as an appetizer, we can say that the last concept among its siblings typically has an incoming edge annotated with a preferred label role set to totalLabel. On the rendering, this is reflected by adding a total line and enhancing the numbers.

Text block pattern

A text block pattern is a specialized hierarchy pattern that only involves a top-level abstract, as well as one nested concept that has a text block type. It is the simplest of all patterns, with all the information it contains being nested in the text block, which can be of any size and can even contain entire pages of text, tables, etc

Network	20000 - Accounting policies

Entity [Axis]	Sample Company
Period [Axis]	Jan. 1 to Dec. 31st, 2010
Language [Axis]	U.S. English

Accounting policies [Abstract]	
Accounting policies [Text Block]	Duis fermentum Sed mauris. Nulla facilisi. Fusce tristique posuere ipsum. Nulla facilisi. Aliquam viverra risus vitae ante. Sed rhoncus mi in wisi. Nullam nibh dui, molestie vitae, imperdiet non, ornare at, elit. • Suspendisse accumsan, arcu vel ornare interdum, magna tellus porta mauris, in porta mi lacus sodales felis. • Phasellus eleifend, diam vitae dapibus pulvinar, erat ligula auctor dui, eget congue justo lorem hendrerit tellus. • Fusce gravida, ligula a placerat placerat, leo erat euismod lectus, et lacinia justo libero non pede. DONEC PULVINAR NONUMMY ERAT Etiam porttitor. Ut venenatis, velit a accumsan interdum, odio metus mollis mauris, non pharetra augue arcu eu felis. Ut eget felis. Mauris leo nulla, sodales et, pharetra quis, fermentum nec, diam.

Figure 5.16: A presentation network using the text block pattern

in XHTML, stored as a single fact. A rendering for the text block pattern is shown on Figure 5.16.

5.9 XML syntax of a presentation linkbase

There is good news: the syntax of a presentation linkbase resembles that of a label linkbase, so that there is not much new to introduce.

5.9.1 Role type definitions

A network is identified by a URI. In the XBRL syntax, this URI is called a link role or a role type. We already saw a link role in Section 4.6.3, with the URI `http://www.xbrl.org/2003/role/l ink`. This is a special, default link role (the only one) that always

```
<xs:schema
  xmlns:xs="http://www.w3.org/2001/XMLSchema"
  xmlns:link="http://www.xbrl.org/2003/linkbase"
  targetNamespace="http://www.xbrlsite.com/DigitalFinancialReporting/
    Metapattern/Hierarchy"
  >

  <xs:annotation>
    <xs:appinfo>
      <link:roleType
        roleURI="http://www.xbrlsite.com/DigitalFinancialReporting/
          Metapattern/Hierarchy/AccountingPolicies"
        id="AccountingPolicies">
        <link:definition>20000 - Accounting Policies</link:definition>
        <link:usedOn>link:presentationLink</link:usedOn>
      </link:roleType>                       Role type definition
    </xs:appinfo>
  </xs:annotation>

</xs:schema>
```

Figure 5.17: A role type definition.

exists. Label linkbases are often defined in this default linkrole, that is, the labels are valid for the entire taxonomy.

For presentation linkbases, link roles allow separating and organizing the concept hierarchies in separate presentation networks.

Each user-defined link role (network identifier) can be defined in a taxonomy schema within the DTS, with a `link:roleType` element, as shown on Figure 5.17. This element is in the `link: annotation` / `link:appinfo` part of the schema. This is the same place where taxonomy schemata also point to linkbases to include in the DTS.

The `roleURI` attribute contains the desired link role URI. Two children elements also exist: `link:definition` is used to optionally associate a user-friendly label with the section. The `link:usedOn` elements specify which linkbases may use this link role. In our case it is only the presentation linkbase. A linkbase is identified with its link name, here `link:presentationLink`.

The role type definition is optional for the default role as long as it is only used on standard linkbases such as presentation linkbases, but it is still useful especially to declare a user-friendly section label. Role type definitions are otherwise required, as well as the default role if used on non-standard linkbases, which is outside of the scope of this chapter.

Presentation networks are associated with a link role using the `xlink:role` attribute, as we will see in the next section.

Label linkbases can also be defined in a different link role than the default link role, by changing the value of the `xlink:role` attribute. In this case, the usual semantics is that label bindings defined in a label linkbase with a non-default link role are only meant to be used for this section. On the other hand, label bindings defined in a label linkbase with the default link role are in scope over the entire DTS.

5.9.2 Presentation links

A presentation linkbase is a DAG of report elements. This means that it is actually simpler than a label linkbase, because both the from and to ends of all arcs are locators pointing to report elements, and no resources are involved.

The only other difference compared to what we explained in Section 4.2.2 are that link names, arc names and arc roles are different.

Presentation link elements

Each presentation network, within a linkbase, is declared with a `link:presentationLink` element, just like a label network is declared with a `link:labelLink element`. This element appears right below a `link:linkbase` element. Yes: we now know two kinds of linkbases and networks: label and presentation. These elements are called presentation links and label links, and their names are called link names. Just like label links, presentation links are extended links in the sense of the XLink standard.

Presentation arcs

Presentation arcs have the name `link:presentationArc`. Their arc roles, that is, the value of their `xlink:arcrole` attribute, is the presentation arc role `http://www.xbrl.org/2003/arcrole/parent-child`. Arc names and arc roles for presentation must be these and we do not advise to change them for interoperability.

There is something new to presentation arcs that label arcs do not have. Presentation arcs are annotated with `preferredLabel` attributes, the value of which is a label role URI.

Ordering arcs in a hierarchy

Furthermore, there is an attribute on arcs that can be used across all linkbases involving hierarchies of report elements such as presentation linkbases: the `order` attribute contains a number with which one can specify the order in which siblings appear under their parent. This number is often an integer, however it can also be a decimal value in order to easily insert new siblings without having to change the `order` attribute of all following siblings every time. Without this attribute (or between edges with the same order value), report elements would appear in an arbitrary order when rendered, which may not correspond to the actual order in the XML syntax.

5.9.3 Spreading a presentation network over multiple files

On the syntactic level, a presentation network could be partitioned across multiple presentation links, over multiple files. We advise against this practice except in the case of extending taxonomies. On the logical perspective, the presentation network used for rendering will be made of all relevant[15] nodes and arcs found across all files in the DTS that are in a presentation link with the desired link role (the network identifier), and with the standardized arc names and arc roles.

5.9.4 Abstract definitions

Abstracts are defined, just like concepts, with XML Schema element declarations. The difference is that:

- the `abstract` attribute is set to true.

- the `type`, `periodType` attributes are semantically irrelevant, but best practices (SEC) are to set them to respectively `xbrl i:stringItemType` and duration. No balances are involved.

---

[15]relevant means after considering arc priorities and overrides, which is an XBRL extensibility mechanism we will introduce later

Chapter 6

Calculation

In the previous chapters, we covered all the basics of XBRL, with which facts can be created, exchanged, validated, and displayed to the end user. The latter leverages model structures, stored in presentation networks.

XBRL, though, supports more than simply displaying facts and checking that, individually, facts are valid against the concept that they are reported against. Indeed, it is also possible to check that groups of facts, together, are valid. The most obvious check is that a group of facts reported against various concepts, sums up to another fact reported against a concept acting as a total.

This is done using calculation networks, which we cover in this chapter. Calculation networks are, besides the presentation network, a very important part of roll-up patterns.

6.1 Validating aggregations of facts

Let us go back to one of the examples given in the previous section: the property, land and equipment network, shown as a reminder on Figure 6.1.

From a presentation perspective, this network is organized with a top-level abstract (Property, plant and equipment [RollUp]), and 6 child concepts.

Taking a closer look at this rendering, one notices three things:

- the top-level abstract is called a roll-up rather than an abstract in the generic sense;

- there is a double line below the bottom-most concept and their associated facts;

- the bottom numbers each correspond to the sums of the five numbers above them.

These properties, as we will see in Section 6.4, define a roll-up pattern.

XBRL provides a way of specifying, in a taxonomy, that there are such constraints in a report. This way, any attempt to produce facts that would not sum up correctly would output an error to the report creator, and, most importantly, a regulatory authority can check each incoming report and reject, early in the process, any report that would not fulfill these constraints. This significantly increases the quality of reports, compared to reports filed in a text processor (such as Word) or in portable document format (PDF).

6.2   Calculation networks

In an XBRL taxonomy, the constraints described in Section 6.1 can be expressed as a calculation linkbase. Like a presentation linkbase, a calculation linkbase is made of trees of report elements. In fact, a calculation linkbase only involves concepts.

The part of a calculation linkbase belonging to a network is called a calculation network. At its tip, there is the concept acting as the main total. The main total has children concepts of which it is the sum, and each child concept may in turn have further

Network	30000 - Property, Plant, and Equipment, by Component
Entity [Axis]	Sample Company
Unit [Axis]	U.S. Dollars

Property, plant and equipment [RollUp]	Period [Axis]	
	Jan. 1 to Dec. 31st, 2009	Jan. 1 to Dec. 31st, 2010
Land	1,147,000	5,347,000
Buildings, net	366,375,000	244,508,000
Furniture and fixtures, net	34,457,000	34,457,000
Computer equipment, net	5,313,000	4,169,000
Other property, plant and equipment, net	6,149,000	6,702,000
Property, plant and equipment, net , total	413,441,000	295,183,000

Figure 6.1: The Property, plant and equipment network

children of which it is a sum. Each non-leaf node in such a tree is thus a roll-up of its children, and this happens on multiple levels.

Figure 6.2 shows the calculation network corresponding to our example. It involves only two levels of concepts, the root and its children. Each edge is annotated with a weight that is a non-zero decimal number. In the vast majority of the cases, for example for accountants, only +1.0 and −1.0 are used, but other weights are in principle allowed. On Figure 6.2, the weight of the edges are shown on the line of each target concept, since there is no ambiguity regarding their parents.

6.3 Balance consistency

In Section 3.6, we explained that concepts are associated with a list of properties such as data type, period type, and balance. We had left the latter aside, and now is the right time to come back to it.

Monetary concepts, that is, concepts that express amounts of money in any currency, are stamped with a balance which can be

Concept	Weight
Property, plant and equipment, net	
Land	+1
Buildings, net	+1
Furniture and fixtures, net	+1
Computer equipment, net	+1
Other property, plant and equipment, net	+1

Figure 6.2: The calculation network for the Property, plant and equipment network. For ease of read, it is displayed using the user-friendly, standard labels.

either *credit* or *debit*. For example, in an income statement, incoming flows like revenues will be modeled as credits, while outbound flows like costs will be modeled as debits. In balance sheets, it is common practice to model assets as debits, and equity as well as liabilities as credits. The same applies to cash flow statements, where cash flows can be credited or debited.

When accountants work on income statements, balance sheets or cash flow statements and check that they sum up, there are a few implicit constraints that always apply:

- credited amounts are added to credited amounts to obtain a new credited amount;

- debited amounts are substracted from credited amounts to obtain a new credited amount;

- debited amounts are added to debited amounts to obtain a new debited amount;

- credited amounts are substracted from debited amounts to obtain a new debited amount.

Concept	Weight
Assets	
Current assets	+1
Assets, Current	+1
Cash, Cash Equivalents, and Short-term Investments	+1
Receivables, Net, Current	+1
Inventory, Net	+1
Inventory, Finished Goods	+1
Inventory for Long-term Contracts or Programs	+1
Inventory, Work in Process	+1
Inventory, Raw Materials	+1
Inventory Valuation Reserves	-1
Inventory, LIFO Reserve	-1
Assets, Noncurrent	+1
Inventory, Noncurrent	+1
Property, Plant and Equipment, Net	+1
Long-term Investments and Receivables, Net	+1
Goodwill	+1
Intangible Assets, Net (Excluding Goodwill)	+1

Figure 6.3: A calculation network involving more levels as well as negative weights (-1). This was obtained by taking an excerpt of the US GAAP taxonomy's balance sheet.

XBRL also enforces such constraints on calculation networks. In any calculation network, the weights on the edges have to be consistent with the above rules:

- an edge connecting two concepts that have the same balance (credit/credit or debit/debit) must have a positive weight;

- an edge connecting two concepts that have opposite balance (credit/debit or debit/credit) must have a negative weight.

Concept	Balance	Weight
Net Income (Loss)	credit	
Income (Loss) from Continuing Operations After Tax	credit	+1
Income (Loss) from Continuing Operations Before Tax	credit	+1
Operating Income (Loss)	credit	+1
Revenues	credit	+1
Costs and Expenses	debit	-1
Cost of Revenue	debit	+1
Operating Expenses	debit	+1
Other Operating Income (Expenses)	credit	+1
Nonoperating Income (Loss)	credit	+1
Interest and Debt Expense	debit	-1
Income (Loss) from Equity Method Investments	credit	+1
Income Tax Expense (Benefit)	debit	-1
Income (Loss) from Discontinued Operations, Net of Tax	credit	+1
Extraordinary Items of Income (Expense), Net of Tax	credit	+1

Figure 6.4: A calculation network fulfilling balance consistency (taken and simplified from Charles Hoffman's fundamental accounting concepts)

An other way to put it, looking at each roll-up structure, is:

- below a credit concept, all children credit concepts are added and all children debit concepts are substracted.

- below a debit concept, all children debit concepts are added and all children credit concepts are substracted.

Figure 6.4 shows a calculation network together with the balance of all the concepts it involves. The reader can check that the above constraints are all fulfilled, which is conformant with XBRL.

6.4   Roll-up patterns

We introduced roll-up patterns in Chapter 5, in addition to hierarchies and text blocks. We have now seen that roll-up patterns do

Concept
Property, plant and equipment, net [RollUp]
Land
Buildings, net
Furniture and fixtures, net
Computer equipment, net
Other property, plant and equipment, net
Property, plant and equipment, net, total

(a) The presentation network (using each preferred label)

Concept	Weight
Property, plant and equipment, net	
Land	+1
Buildings, net	+1
Furniture and fixtures, net	+1
Computer equipment, net	+1
Other property, plant and equipment, net	+1

(b) The calculation network (displayed here with standard labels)

Figure 6.5: The presentation and calculation networks that the Property, plant and equipment network encompasses.

not only involve presentation, but also calculations.

In terms of networks: a network that constitutes a roll-up pattern is made of a presentation network and a calculation network (leaving aside the label linkbase that usually goes across all networks).

Going back to our roll-up example, as can be seen on Figure 6.6, these two networks are not quite the same, even though they share some of their structure.

6.4.1   XBRL standard, regulatory constraints, and common practices

XBRL specifies what calculation linkbases and presentation linkbases are made of (in particular: weights, preferred labels, etc), but how these linkbases interact together, if and how they are consistent with each other in some way, and how they are structured across networks is left to common practices.

Often, regulatory authorities do impose such consistencies to their filers, but companies also tend to stick to some common practices that established themselves in the past few years. It is these common practices that Charles Hoffman investigated and summarized as patterns. Based on this, one can *recommend* to the filers to follow these common practices to enhance quality and comparability of filings.

It is to be noted that these patterns apply to presentation-based taxonomies and not to DPM-based taxonomies.

6.4.2   Strict roll-up consistency

We start by showing how a strict roll-up consistency between presentation and calculation looks like. Ideally, filers filing according to a network partitioning models should stick to these strict consistency rules.

Simple roll-ups

Let us begin with a simple roll-up that does not involve any nesting, such as the Property, plant and equipment network, shown again on Figure 6.5 placing the presentation network and calculation network next to each other. It can be seen that in the calculation network, the root is the concept that expresses the total, and its children are the operands of the aggregation: only concepts are involved.

Concept
Property, plant and equipment, net [RollUp]
Land
Buildings, net
Furniture and fixtures, net
Computer equipment, net
Other property, plant and equipment, net
Property, plant and equipment, net, total

Concept
Property, plant and equipment, net
+ Land
+ Buildings, net
+ Furniture and fixtures, net
+ Computer equipment, net
+ Other property, plant and equipment, net

(a) The presentation network

(b) The calculation network (weights marked on the left)

Figure 6.6: The presentation and calculation networks that the Property, plant and equipment network encompasses.

In the presentation network, the operands are also siblings, and in the same order. In this respect, the two networks are alike. However, there are two major differences.

First, in the presentation network, the total concept appears not as the root, but as an additional sibling at the bottom, last child. Furthermore, this concept, which has the underlying SQName `pattern:PropertyPlantAndEquipmentNet`, is associated with a preferred label totalLabel. This is why this concept is displayed as "Property, plant and equipment, net" (standard label) in calculation, but as "Property, plant and equipment, net, total" in presentation (note that it is our own editorial choice to use standard labels for calculation, just to isolate the reader from internal SQNames at this point for ease of read).

Second, the root is an abstract that bears a similar name to the total concept, that is, it often uses the same SQName with an `Abstract` suffix, and a similar label to the total concept's standard label, but with an additional [RollUp] or [Abstract] stamp like all abstracts (recall that label roles do not make sense for abstracts, so that only the standard label is really useful).

Nested roll-ups

Now, let us take at look at how these structural constraints are generalized for nested roll-ups. We have already seen how nested roll-ups are modeled in calculation networks. It is quite straightforward: each concept can itself have further children concepts of which it is the aggregate.

In the presentation network, in order to nest a roll-up in lieu of a leaf concept, this leaf concept is merely replaced with the presentation structure corresponding to its simple roll-up as explained previously. That is, it is replaced with the abstract report element, under which all operands appear, as well as the original leaf concept at the last child, with totalLabel as a preferred label role.

Figure 6.7 shows, as an example, the presentation network next to the calculation network for the previously shown income statement, which involves nested roll-ups.

Note that the label roles of the non-total concepts can deviate. For example, negative labels can be used, like "Loss (Income)" instead of "Income (Loss)" for an easier read when lots of numbers are negative. Also, terser labels can be used.

6.4.3   Relaxed roll-up consistency

A significant number of filers use a more relaxed consistency compared to what we showed in the previous section.

Total labels

In practice, some filers omit the use of totalLabels as preferred label roles in presentation networks to mark total concepts as such. Concretely, this means that they use the standard label role although it actually contains the word "total." From a data processing perspective, this is of no consequence, as the roll-up pattern can still

Concept

Net Income (Loss) [RollUp]
  Income (Loss) from Continuing Operations After Tax [RollUp]
    Income (Loss) from Continuing Operations Before Tax [RollUp]
      Operating Income (Loss) [RollUp]
        Revenues
        Costs and Expenses [RollUp]
          Cost of Revenue
          Operating Expenses
          Costs and Expenses
        Other Operating Income (Expenses)
        Operating Income (Loss)
      Nonoperating Income (Loss)
      Interest and Debt Expense
      Income (Loss) from Equity Method Investments
      Income (Loss) from Continuing Operations Before Tax
    Income Tax Expense (Benefit)
    Income (Loss) from Continuing Operations After Tax
  Income (Loss) from Discontinued Operations, Net of Tax
  Extraordinary Items of Income (Expense), Net of Tax
  Net Income (Loss)

(a) The presentation network (using each preferred label)

Concept

Net Income (Loss)
  + Income (Loss) from Continuing Operations After Tax
    + Income (Loss) from Continuing Operations Before Tax
      + Operating Income (Loss)
        + Revenues
        - Costs and Expenses
          + Cost of Revenue
          + Operating Expenses
        + Other Operating Income (Expenses)
      + Nonoperating Income (Loss)
      - Interest and Debt Expense
      + Income (Loss) from Equity Method Investments
    - Income Tax Expense (Benefit)
  + Income (Loss) from Discontinued Operations, Net of Tax
  + Extraordinary Items of Income (Expense), Net of Tax

(b) The calculation network (displayed here with standard labels)

Figure 6.7: The presentation and calculation networks that the income statement encompasses.

Concept

Net Income (Loss) [RollUp]
  Income (Loss) from Continuing Operations After Tax [RollUp]
    Income (Loss) from Continuing Operations Before Tax [RollUp]
      Revenues
      Cost of Revenue
      Operating Expenses
      Costs and Expenses
      Other Operating Income (Expenses)
      Operating Income (Loss)
      Nonoperating Income (Loss)
      Interest and Debt Expense
      Income (Loss) from Equity Method Investments
      Income (Loss) from Continuing Operations Before Tax
    Income Tax Expense (Benefit)
    Income (Loss) from Continuing Operations After Tax
  Income (Loss) from Discontinued Operations, Net of Tax
  Extraordinary Items of Income (Expense), Net of Tax
  Net Income (Loss)

Figure 6.8: A relaxed presentation network for our income statement example. Some nested roll-ups were flattened, omitting the wrapping abstracts.

be inferred from the calculation network. However, it is very advisable to use totalLabels for clarity.

Flattened nested roll-ups

A very significant number of filers do not use abstract report elements for each nested roll-up, because this can lead to very verbose presentation networks. The end user sees the flat, nested roll-ups as intermediate totals, because they appear under a single or double line.

Note that, even if roll-ups get flattened in this way, it is still paramount that the calculation network is consistent with the presentation network, that is, that they would have been strictly consistent with each other if these roll-up abstracts had been present.

Although this is an established practice, we advise adhering to the strict roll-up pattern, using an abstract element to wrap around each nested roll-up. Making the displayed network easier to read for the end user should be done by the application facing the end-user (which can omit displaying these abstracts) rather than in the underlying structure.

6.5 XML syntax of a calculation linkbase

The good news about the XML syntax of a calculation linkbase is that 95% of it was already introduced in the previous chapters. From a syntactic perspective, a calculation linkbase is a graph of concepts, and looks exactly like a presentation linkbase. Only some names change, and the weight attribute is introduced.

Typically, the presentation linkbase and the label linkbase will each be stored in their own XML file, and the calculation linkbase will get its own file as well. Calculation linkbases can be embedded in taxonomy schema files as well, in the same way as any other linkbase. Calculation linkbases are linked from schemata or other linkbases in the same way as any linkbase (see Section 4.6.8).

6.5.1 Link names, arc names and arc roles

Let us start with a quick reminder. Label linkbases use the link name `link:labelLink`, the arc name `link:labelArc` and the arc role `http://www.xbrl.org/2003/arcrole/concept-label`. Presentation linkbases use the link name `link:presentationLink`, the arc name `link:presentationArc` and the arc role `http://www.xbrl.org/2003/arcrole/parent-child`.

Calculation linkbases use their own names and roles as well:

- `link:calculationLink` for the link name;

- `link:calculationArc` for the arc names;

- `http://www.xbrl.org/2003/arcrole/summation-item` for the arc role.

.

Link roles are used in the same way, meaning that they are network identifiers (URIs).

6.5.2　Weight attribute

In a calculation linkbase, each arc, i.e., each `link:calculationArc` element, must contain a new `weight` attribute, which contains a non-zero decimal value, and that is the weight used for the aggregation. It goes without saying that `preferredLabel` attributes only apply to presentation linkbases and cannot be used on calculation linkbases.

Chapter 7

Hypercubes

We have so far covered the basics of XBRL. We saw builtin aspects: concept, entity, period, unit, language. We saw two kinds of report elements: concepts and abstracts. We saw how they can be organized in presentation structures and associated with user-friendly labels.

While reports can be created with XBRL using only the above knowledge, it becomes quickly clear that sticking to these builtin aspects doesn't bring us very far. For example, in a sales report, it is desirable to break up by products or by countries.

Such use cases require the introduction of more aspects than just the five builtin aspects: user-defined aspects. XBRL allows this by the means of dimensions. This chapter introduces dimensions.

7.1 More on the cubic data model of XBRL

Let us start with good news: the data model that we introduced in Chapter 2 remains the same: we merely add further aspects.

Aspect	Characteristic
Concept	Director, Salary
Entity	Sample Company
Period	January 1, 2017 to December 31, 2017
Unit	U.S. Dollars
Director	Jane Doe
Fact value	1,000

Figure 7.1: A fact with a user-defined aspect (Director) and its associated value (Jane Doe). This aspect is important, because it indicates that the specified salary applies to a specific employee of Sample Company.

7.1.1   Facts with extra aspects

Figure 7.1 shows a fact that has an extra aspect, that is, beyond the standard aspects introduced in Chapter 2. This fact is taken from a sample by Charles Hoffman. Facts can have more than one extra aspect, that is, there is no limitation on how many aspects a fact can have. Figure 7.2 shows a real fact from an EDGAR filing that has three user-defined aspects. Both figures represent the facts using user-friendly labels, but we will soon dive into the machinery behind them.

Aspect	Characteristic
Concept	New Accounting Pronouncement or Change in Accounting Principle, Effect of Adoption, Quantification
Entity	Coca Cola, Inc.
Period	January 1, 2016 to December 31, 2016
Unit	U.S. Dollars
Adjustments for New Accounting Pronouncements [Axis]	Accounting Standards Update 2015-17 [Member]
Income Statement Location [Axis]	Income Statement Location [Domain]
Balance Sheet Location [Axis]	Prepaid Expenses and Other Current Assets [Member]
Fact value	80,000,000

Figure 7.2: A fact with three user-defined aspects, taken from a real EDGAR filing by Coca Cola. We omit the precision (-6).

7.1.2   Dimensions and Members

As can be seen on Figure 7.2, the extra aspects and associated values, which we represented with user-friendly labels in English, have these square brackets "[Axis]", "[Member]" and "[Domain]", which is common practice with the US GAAP taxonomy and many other presentation-based taxonomies around the world. This will probably remind the reader of similar square brackets in labels for Abstracts ("[Abstract]", "[RollUp]", and so on).

In fact, this is because these three user-defined aspects are report elements, like abstracts and concepts, which we are already familiar with. Likewise the associated values are report elements, too[1]. Like any report elements, they have internal SQNames. Let us look again at the real fact of Figure 7.2, but looking at the underlying SQNames as shown on Figure 7.3.

Dimensions

The three new aspects (`us-gaap:AdjustmentsForNewAccountin gPronouncementsAxis`, `us-gaap:IncomeStatementLocationAxis` and `us-gaap:BalanceSheetLocationAxis`) correspond to a new type of report elements called dimensions. In US-GAAP-like taxonomies, dimensions have SQNames that end with `Axis` by convention. Like concepts and abstracts, dimensions can be associated with labels, using the exact same machinery (language, label role, etc) and, likewise, these labels are suffixed with "[Axis]" for clarity to the end user.

Members

The three associated values `us-gaap:AccountingStandardsUpdat e201517Member`, `us-gaap:IncomeStatementLocationDomain` and

---

[1]For explicit dimensions. They can also be atomic values, as we will see later for typed dimensions.

Aspect	Characteristic
Concept	us-gaap:NewAccountingPronouncementOrChangeInAccountingPrincipleEffectOfAdoptionQuantification
Entity	Coca Cola, Inc.
Period	2016-01-01/2016-12-31
Unit	ISO4217:USD
us-gaap:AdjustmentsForNewAccountingPronouncementsAxis	us-gaap:AccountingStandardsUpdate201517Member
us-gaap:IncomeStatementLocationAxis	us-gaap:IncomeStatementLocationDomain
us-gaap:BalanceSheetLocationAxis	us-gaap:PrepaidExpensesAndOtherCurrentAssetsMember
Fact value	80,000,000

Figure 7.3: A fact with three user-defined aspects, taken from a real EDGAR filing by Coca Cola. We show the internal SQNames.

`us-gaap:PrepaidExpensesAndOtherCurrentAssetsMember`) correspond to a new type of report elements called members. In US-
GAAP-like taxonomies, members have SQNames that end with
`Member` or `Domain` (we will explain the difference later). Like concepts, abstracts and dimensions, members can be associated with
labels, using the exact same machinery (language, label role, etc)
and, likewise, these labels are suffixed with "[Member]" or "[Do-
main]" for clarity to the end user.

To summarize, we now know four different kinds of report elements: concepts, abstracts, dimensions and members. All are displayed to the end user with user-friendly labels in the appropriate
language.

7.1.3   Explicit or typed dimensions

In the examples we have seen so far, facts associate each dimension,
that is, a user-defined aspect, with a member. Built-in aspects are
special and as we have seen, the concept aspect is associated with
a concept, the period aspect with an instant period or duration,
the unit aspect with a unit SQName.

Dimensions that are associated with members are called explicit
dimensions. In XBRL, there also exists dimensions that are typed
dimensions (such as integer, date, etc)[2], and that are associated
with a value from the value space of that type. The main difference
is that explicit dimensions have a value space that is explicitly
defined as a list of possible members, while typed dimensions have
a potentially infinite value space.

---

[2]Technically, the type system used to define typed dimensions in XBRL
is based on XML Schema elements, which means that the types can also be
structured (complex types). It is, however, recommended to stick to simple
types, and if possible, pre-defined types. This keeps the XBRL data model
completely independent from that of XML. Using complex XML Schema types
will only confuse the end users. You can think of this practice as a kind of first
normal form.

7.1.4 Fact tables

Even with these further aspects, facts still have a tabular nature, and can be displayed in fact tables – but the fact tables will now start to have extra columns that the user can introduce themselves, on top of the five builtin ones. Figure 7.4 shows a fact table with an extra aspect.

To be more precise, facts are organized in hypercubes. Hypercubes are like cubes, except that they can have more dimensions than the three we are used to in our world. We call these dimensions aspects[3], as was explained in Chapter 2.

Even with what we have seen so far in Chapter 2, hypercubes were already there, but only implicitly – we just did not say the word. We used the notion of networks to group facts together meaningfully. And these implicit hypercubes already had five dimensions, that we called aspects: concept, entity, period, unit, language. Most of the time, some of these aspects may be missing: numeric facts do not have a language aspect, and textual facts do not have units for example. This leaves only four aspects in most networks.

---

[3]and the term "dimension" is usually used for user-defined aspects.

Concept	Entity	Period	Unit	Director [Axis]	Value
Directors, Salary	Sample Company	January 1, 2017 thru December 31, 2017	U.S. Dollars	Jane Doe [Member]	1,000
Directors, Bonus	Sample Company	January 1, 2017 thru December 31, 2017	U.S. Dollars	Jane Doe [Member]	1,000
Directors, Fee	Sample Company	January 1, 2017 thru December 31, 2017	U.S. Dollars	Jane Doe [Member]	1,000
Directors, Options Granted, at Fair Value	Sample Company	January 1, 2017 thru December 31, 2017	U.S. Dollars	Jane Doe [Member]	1,000
Directors, Salary	Sample Company	January 1, 2017 thru December 31, 2017	U.S. Dollars	John Doe [Member]	1,000
Directors, Bonus	Sample Company	January 1, 2017 thru December 31, 2017	U.S. Dollars	John Doe [Member]	1,000
Directors, Fee	Sample Company	January 1, 2017 thru December 31, 2017	U.S. Dollars	John Doe [Member]	1,000
Directors, Options Granted, at Fair Value	Sample Company	January 1, 2017 thru December 31, 2017	U.S. Dollars	John Doe [Member]	1,000
Directors, Salary	Sample Company	January 1, 2017 thru December 31, 2017	U.S. Dollars	All directors [Domain]	2,000
Directors, Bonus	Sample Company	January 1, 2017 thru December 31, 2017	U.S. Dollars	All directors [Domain]	2,000
Directors, Fee	Sample Company	January 1, 2017 thru December 31, 2017	U.S. Dollars	All directors [Domain]	2,000
Directors, Options Granted, at Fair Value	Sample Company	January 1, 2017 thru December 31, 2017	U.S. Dollars	All directors [Domain]	2,000

Figure 7.4: A fact table, displaying several textual facts in structured form, one fact per row. Notice the user-defined aspect Director, a dimension, as well as its three members Jane Doe, John Doe and All directors.

7.2 Networks and hypercubes

In Chapter 5, we introduced networks and showed how networks can be used to group facts in meaningful units: for example, a network can be a balance sheet, an income statement, and so on.

A network can be split into several hypercubes, that we call components. A component is thus identified with a network identifier, and a hypercube name.

A possible source of confusion is that the name of the hypercube alone is not enough, because a hypercube name may be reused in another network. In EDGAR filings, it is very often the case that different networks reuse the same hypercube (or table, as they are called in US-GAAP-like taxonomies) name. The most prominent example is the "Statement [Table]" hypercube, whose SQName is `us-gaap:StatementTable`. Coca Cola commonly uses this hypercube name in the balance sheet network, the income statement network and the cash flow network. Some filers do choose, however, to have the discipline to have unique hypercube names without reusing them across networks, so that it is also not a universal practice, but something to be aware of when developing XBRL software or dealing with XBRL data with presentation-based taxonomies.

The bottomline is: one needs a network identifier together with a hypercube name to identify a component, but the really best practice is to nevertheless use unique hypercube names[4].

7.2.1 Implicit hypercube

A network can thus be partitioned in several components. One of these components has the particularity of not being associated with any hypercube name: this hypercube with no name is the implicit hypercube.

---

[4]This best practice does not apply to DPM-based taxonomies.

In the previous chapters, all our networks had only one component with no hypercube name: the implicit hypercube. Facts that
are in this component cannot have any user-defined aspects: they
only have the built-in aspects that we described in Chapter 2^5.

In general, networks can have several components, and one of
these components may be associated with the implicit hypercube
while the others have named hypercubes.

It is best practice, and advisable, to not use implicit hypercubes[6], that is, to always define hypercube names in each network.
The remainder of this chapter explains how to design networks to
do so. We will start with redesigning the networks encountered
in Chapter 5 by replacing the implicit hypercubes with explicitly
named hypercubes. Later on, we will then show how (named) hypercubes can be extended with user-defined aspects.

It is also recommended, for even cleaner reports, to further
restrict the design and have only one component per network. In
summary, the overall recommendation is: each network has one
named hypercube – and thus one component – and this hypercube
has a unique name across networks[7]. However, it is also important
to understand the semantics of an XBRL report for which these
conditions do not hold, i.e., to be able to process reports in which
networks may contain several hypercubes among which an implicit
hypercube, and in which hypercube names may be reused across
networks. This is something that, in spite of this recommendation,
is encountered often in practice in presentation-based reports.

---

[5]Some reporting authorities, though, do enrich on the logical level all hypercubes, including implicit hypercubes, with implicit aspects. For example,
the SEC defines an aspect called the legal entity, and assumes that all facts
that do not say otherwise apply to the Consolidated Entity. From a data modelling perspective, this really is the same as actually having this extra aspect,
always, and thus assuming that implicit hypercubes have it as well.

[6]This also applies to DPM-based reports.

[7]This best practice does not apply to DPM-based taxonomies.

7.2.2 Hypercube report elements

A hypercube is a new kind of report element, like concepts and abstracts, like dimensions and members. Like them, it thus has a name which is an SQName, for example `us-gaap:StatementT able` or `us-gaap:ScheduleOfTradingSecuritiesAndOtherTradi ngAssetsTable`. Also like them, it can be associated with user-friendly labels in various languages. In the US GAAP taxonomy, labels end with "[Table]" to make clear that they are hypercubes. You may remember that this convention to end labels with a term in square brackets was already encountered for abstracts ("[Abstract]"). Likewise, the SQNames of hypercubes end with `Table`, just like abstracts end with `Abstract`.

In a presentation network, the hypercube appears above the hierarchy of abstracts and concepts[8]. In our previous example of Chapter 5, presentation networks only contained abstracts and concepts, meaning that the network had one implicit hypercube, also called an implied table. Even though this practice of using implicit hypercubes is widespread, XBRL international recommends not doing so, and always making hypercubes explicit. Figure 7.5 shows the presentation networks for our two previous examples (Plant, Property and Equipment as well as Accounting Policies), where the hypercube is made explicit. Figures 7.6 and 7.7 show the updated renderings, where an extra header can be seen that shows the hypercube name in addition to the network. If the hypercube is implicit (i.e., the presentation networks from Chapter 5), then "Implied Table [Table]" typically appears instead of the name of the explicit hypercube.

Note that it is very common, even though semantically useless, to add one more abstract on top of the hypercube to wrap it. The reason is simply that, this way, it is also possible for several hypercubes to appear under that abstract, in the same network.

---

[8]This does not apply to taxonomies based on the DPM, which use table linkbases instead of presentation linkbases to organize facts.

20000 - Accounting Policies

Report element	Kind	Type	Period Type
Accounting policies [Abstract]	Abstract	-	-
Accounting policies [Table]	Hypercube	-	-
Accounting policies [Hierarchy]	Abstract	-	-
Basis of presentation	Concept	Text block	instant
Trade receivables policy	Concept	Text block	instant
Inventory policies [Abstract]	Abstract	-	-
Inventory valuation method	Concept	Text block	instant
Description of inventory components	Concept	Text block	instant
Inventory cost method	Concept	Text block	instant
Investments in securities policy	Concept	Text block	instant
Bank borrowing policy	Concept	Text block	instant
Provisions policy	Concept	Text block	instant

(a) The accounting policies

30000 - Property, Plant, and Equipment, by Component

Report element	Kind	Type	Balance	Period Type
Property, plant and equipment [Abstract]	Abstract	-	-	-
Property, plant and equipment [Table]	Hypercube	-	-	-
Property, plant and equipment [Roll Up]	Abstract	-	-	-
Land	Concept	Monetary	debit	instant
Buildings, net	Concept	Monetary	debit	instant
Furniture and fixtures, net	Concept	Monetary	debit	instant
Computer equipment, net	Concept	Monetary	debit	instant
Other property, plant and equipment, net	Concept	Monetary	debit	instant
Property, plant and equipment, net	Concept	Monetary	debit	instant

(b) The Property, plant and equipment

Figure 7.5: The presentation linkbases, displayed in a user-friendly fashion using labels, and making the hypercube explicit.

Having several hypercubes in the same network is a bit rarer, but does happen in many EDGAR filings although, as we explained earlier, this is not recommended. We do recommend, however, to nevertheless always have this top-level abstract.

Network	20000 - Accounting Policies
Hypercube	Accounting policies [Table]

Entity [Axis]	Sample Company
Period [Axis]	Jan. 1 to Dec. 31st, 2010
Language [Axis]	U.S. English

Accounting policies [Hierarchy]	
Basis of presentation	Praesent fringilla feugiat magna. Suspendisse et lorem eu risus convallis placerat.Suspendisse potenti. Donec malesuada loremid mi. Nunc ut purus ac nisl tempus accumsan.
Trade receivables policy	Sed magna felis, accumsan a, fermentum quis, varius sed, ipsum. Nullam leo. Donec eros.
Inventory policies [Abstract]	
Inventory valuation method	Cost
Description of inventory components	Proin elit sem, ornare non, ullamcorper vel, sollicitudin a, lacus. Mauris tincidunt cursus est. Nulla sit amet nibh. Sed elementum feugiat augue. Nam
Inventory cost method	FIFO
Investments in securities policy	Etiam ipsum orci, gravida nec, feugiat ut, malesuada quis, mauris. Etiam porttitor. Ut venenatis, velit a accumsan interdum, odio metus mollis mauris, non pharetra augue arcu eu felis.
Bank borrowing policy	Ut ut risus nec nibh dictum posuere. Phasellus eleifend, diam vitae dapibus pulvinar, erat ligula auctor dui, eget conguejusto lorem hendrerit tellus.
Provisions policy	vestibulum augue eu justo. Pellentesque habitant morbi tristique senectus et netus et malesuada fames ac turpis egestas.

Figure 7.6: The renderings corresponding to the new accounting policies presentation network, making the hypercube explicit.

Network	30000 - Property, Plant, and Equipment, by Component
Hypercube	Property, plant and equipment [Table]

Entity [Axis]	Sample Company
Unit [Axis]	U.S. Dollars

Property, plant and equipment [Abstract]	Period [Axis]	
	Jan. 1 to Dec. 31st, 2009	Jan. 1 to Dec. 31st, 2010
Land	1,147,000	5,347,000
Buildings, net	366,375,000	244,508,000
Furniture and fixtures, net	34,457,000	34,457,000
Computer equipment, net	5,313,000	4,169,000
Other property, plant and equipment, net	6,149,000	6,702,000
Property, plant and equipment, net	413,441,000	295,183,000

Figure 7.7: The renderings corresponding to the new PPE presentation networks, making the hypercube explicit.

7.2.3   Line-items report elements

The report element right below a hypercube, in a presentation network, is called a line-items report element. This is our sixth and last kind of report element. It bears this name because in accounting, the concepts listed below it are called line items. To avoid confusion, we will always call this wrapping explicitly a line-items report element.

Figure 7.8 shows our two networks with this one more report element. Our networks are now complete with an explicit hypercube and an explicit line-items report element. Figures 7.9 and 7.10 show the updated renderings.

Strictly speaking, in XBRL terms, a line-items report element is not really distinguishable from an abstract. It is actually syntactically an abstract, and what makes it a line-items report element is only that it appears right between the hypercube and the hierarchy of concepts and abstracts in a presentation network.

However, from a data modelling perspective, we recommend making use of line-items report elements explicitly, that is, giving them SQNames ending with `LineItems` and user-friendly labels ending with "[Line Items]" or the appropriate translation, as is done in the US GAAP taxonomy.

20000 - Accounting Policies

Report element	Kind	Type	Period Type
Accounting policies [Abstract]	Abstract	-	-
Accounting policies [Table]	Hypercube	-	-
Accounting policies [Line Items]	LineItems	-	-
Accounting policies [Hierarchy]	Abstract	-	-
Basis of presentation	Concept	Text block	instant
Trade receivables policy	Concept	Text block	instant
Inventory policies [Abstract]	Abstract	-	-
Inventory valuation method	Concept	Text block	instant
Description of inventory components	Concept	Text block	instant
Inventory cost method	Concept	Text block	instant
Investments in securities policy	Concept	Text block	instant
Bank borrowing policy	Concept	Text block	instant
Provisions policy	Concept	Text block	instant

(a) The accounting policies

30000 - Property, Plant, and Equipment, by Component

Report element	Kind	Type	Balance	Period Type
Property, plant and equipment [Abstract]	Abstract	-	-	-
Property, plant and equipment [Table]	Hypercube	-	-	-
Property, plant and equipment [Line Items]	LineItems	-	-	-
Property, plant and equipment [Roll Up]	Abstract	-	-	-
Land	Concept	Monetary	debit	instant
Buildings, net	Concept	Monetary	debit	instant
Furniture and fixtures, net	Concept	Monetary	debit	instant
Computer equipment, net	Concept	Monetary	debit	instant
Other property, plant and equipment, net	Concept	Monetary	debit	instant
Property, plant and equipment, net	Concept	Monetary	debit	instant

(b) The Property, plant and equipment

Figure 7.8: The presentation linkbases, displayed in a user-friendly fashion using labels, and using line-items report elements between the hypercube and the hierarchy of abstracts and concepts.

Network	20000 - Accounting Policies
Hypercube	Accounting policies [Table]

Entity [Axis]	Sample Company
Period [Axis]	Jan. 1 to Dec. 31st, 2010
Language [Axis]	U.S. English

Accounting policies [Line Items]	
Accounting policies [Hierarchy]	
Basis of presentation	Praesent fringilla feugiat magna. Suspendisse et lorem eu risus convallis placerat.Suspendisse potenti. Donec malesuada loremid mi. Nunc ut purus ac nisl tempus accumsan.
Trade receivables policy	Sed magna felis, accumsan a, fermentum quis, varius sed, ipsum. Nullam leo. Donec eros.
Inventory policies [Abstract]	
Inventory valuation method	Cost
Description of inventory components	Proin elit sem, ornare non, ullamcorper vel, sollicitudin a, lacus. Mauris tincidunt cursus est. Nulla sit amet nibh. Sed elementum feugiat augue. Nam
Inventory cost method	FIFO
Investments in securities policy	Etiam ipsum orci, gravida nec, feugiat ut, malesuada quis, mauris. Etiam porttitor. Ut venenatis, velit a accumsan interdum, odio metus mollis mauris, non pharetra augue arcu eu felis.
Bank borrowing policy	Ut ut risus nec nibh dictum posuere. Phasellus eleifend, diam vitae dapibus pulvinar, erat ligula auctor dui, eget conguejusto lorem hendrerit tellus.
Provisions policy	vestibulum augue eu justo. Pellentesque habitant morbi tristique senectus et netus et malesuada fames ac turpis egestas.

Figure 7.9: The renderings corresponding to the new accounting policies presentation network, making the line-items report element explicit.

Network	30000 - Property, Plant, and Equipment, by Component
Hypercube	Property, plant and equipment [Table]

Entity [Axis]	Sample Company
Unit [Axis]	U.S. Dollars

Property, plant and equipment [Line Items]	Period [Axis]	
	Jan. 1 to Dec. 31st, 2009	Jan. 1 to Dec. 31st, 2010
Property, plant and equipment [Roll Up]		
Land	1,147,000	5,347,000
Buildings, net	366,375,000	244,508,000
Furniture and fixtures, net	34,457,000	34,457,000
Computer equipment, net	5,313,000	4,169,000
Other property, plant and equipment, net	6,149,000	6,702,000
Property, plant and equipment, net	413,441,000	295,183,000

Figure 7.10: The renderings corresponding to the new PPE presentation networks, making the line-items report element explicit.

7.2.4 Presenting hypercubes with explicit dimensions

Now that we have all report elements in place (concepts, abstracts, dimensions, members, hypercubes and line-items report elements), we have all the building blocks we need to assemble a presentation network that models a hypercube with user-defined explicit dimensions. We leave typed dimensions outside of the discussion for now[9]. We also stick to networks that have a unique hypercube for now: to build a presentation network with several components, it suffices to put several hypercube report elements, and their subtrees, below the top-level abstract. Of course, for a network with several components, one will only typically display one component[10] at a time.

In the previous section, we have already built presentation networks with explicit hypercubes, but have not yet made use of any extra dimensions. This is what we will be doing now.

Figure 7.11 shows the presentation network within a network that has an explicit hypercube with extra dimensions. Dimensions, in this case only one, are directly nested below the hypercube. Members, that is, possible values that the dimension can take, are then organized in a hierarchy below each dimension. A hierarchy of members below a dimension is called a domain. This is why a top-level member is often called a domain[11], and its label is suffixed with "[Domain]" in the US GAAP taxonomy.

The fact table corresponding to this network was already shown earlier, on Figure 7.4.

---

[9]Typed dimensions are not allowed in EDGAR filings, but some reporting authorities do use them.

[10]Reminder: hypercube within a network.

[11]This is because, formally, we typically identify the top-level member with the aggregation of the entire member hierarchy. This will be explained later with default members.

50000 - Director Compensation

Report element	Kind	Type	Period Type
Director Compensation [Abstract]	Abstract	-	-
Director Compensation [Table]	Hypercube	-	-
Director [Axis]	Dimension	-	-
All directors [Domain]	Member	-	-
John Doe [Member]	Member	-	-
Jane Doe [Member]	Member	-	-
Director Compensation [Line Items]	LineItems	-	-
Director Compensation [Hierarchy]	Abstract	-	-
Director, Salary	Concept	Monetary	instant
Director, Bonus	Concept	Monetary	instant
Director, Fee	Concept	Monetary	instant
Director, Options Granted, at Fair Value	Concept	Monetary	instant

(a) The director compensation presentation network, with standard labels

http://www.xbrlsite.com/DigitalFinancialReporting/Metapattern/CompoundFact/DirectorCompensation

Report element	Kind	Type	Period Type
pattern:DirectorCompensationAbstract	Abstract	-	-
pattern:DirectorCompensationTable	Hypercube	-	-
pattern:DirectorAxis	Dimension	-	-
pattern:AllDirectorsDomain	Member	-	-
pattern:JohnDoeMember	Member	-	-
pattern:JaneDoeMember	Member	-	-
pattern:DirectorCompensationLineItems	LineItems	-	-
pattern:DirectorCompensationHierarchy	Abstract	-	-
pattern:DirectorSalary	Concept	xbrli:monetaryItemType	instant
pattern:DirectorBonus	Concept	xbrli:monetaryItemType	instant
pattern:DirectorFee	Concept	xbrli:monetaryItemType	instant
pattern:DirectorOptionsGrantedAtFairValue	Concept	xbrli:monetaryItemType	instant

(b) The director compensation presentation network, with SQNames and the network identifier

Figure 7.11: The director compensation presentation network, which demonstrates how dimensions and members fit in a presentation network under a hypercube. It is shown once using user-friendly labels, and once using raw SQNames.

Network	5000 - Director Compensation
Hypercube	Director Compensation [Table]

Entity [Axis]	Sample Company
Period [Axis]	Jan. 1 to Dec. 31st, 2010
Unit [Axis]	U.S. Dollars

	Director [Axis]		
	All directors [Domain]		
Director Compensation [Line Items]	John Doe [Member]	Jane Doe [Member]	
Director Compensation [Hierarchy]			
Director, Salary	1'000	1'000	2'000
Director, Bonus	1'000	1'000	2'000
Director, Fee	1'000	1'000	2'000
Director, Options Granted, at Fair Value	1'000	1'000	2'000

Figure 7.12: The renderings corresponding to the director compensation presentation network, with dimensions and members.

Figure 7.12 shows the corresponding rendering. Since there is only one period in this case, the period aspect appears together with the unit axis and the entity axis on top of the rendering. The dimension representing the directors appears on the columns. Notice how the third column, with the top-level member (domain), is shaped as an L and wraps up its two child members. These L shapes are very common on XBRL reports.

Figures 7.13 and 7.14 show alternate renderings where the period axis appears as a column header as well, or where the members appear on rows and line items on columns. In the latter rendering, there is no L shape, because the hierarchy abstract and the line-items report element are not concepts, and thus no fact can be reported against them. If, however, the hierarchy of line items were a roll-up pattern and were displayed on the columns, then L-shaped cells could be used as well for every global or intermediate total.

Network	5000 - Director Compensation		
Hypercube	Director Compensation [Table]		
Entity [Axis]	Sample Company		
Unit [Axis]	U.S. Dollars		

	Period [Axis]		
	Jan. 1 to Dec. 31st, 2010		
	Director [Axis]		
	All directors [Domain]		
Director Compensation [Line Items]	John Doe [Member]	Jane Doe [Member]	
Director Compensation [Hierarchy]			
Director, Salary	1'000	1'000	2'000
Director, Bonus	1'000	1'000	2'000
Director, Fee	1'000	1'000	2'000
Director, Options Granted, at Fair Value	1'000	1'000	2'000

Figure 7.13: An alternate rendering of the director compensation network, with the period displayed as a column header.

Network	5000 - Director Compensation			
Hypercube	Director Compensation [Table]			
Entity [Axis]	Sample Company			
Period [Axis]	Jan. 1 to Dec. 31st, 2010			
Unit [Axis]	U.S. Dollars			

	Director Compensation [Line Items]			
	Director Compensation [Hierarchy]			
Director [Axis]	Director, Salary	Director, Bonus	Director, Fee	Director, Options Granted, at Fair Value
John Doe [Member]	1'000	1'000	1'000	1'000
Jane Doe [Member]	1'000	1'000	1'000	1'000
All directors [Domain]	2'000	2'000	2'000	2'000

Figure 7.14: An alternate rendering of the director compensation network, with members as rows and line items as columns.

7.3   Dimension hierarchies

Let us now dive a bit more into dimension hierarchies. There are a few constraints in which our model structure (presentation network) is organized. Dimensions must appear under hypercubes, and members must appear below either a dimension, or below other members (recursively).

7.3.1   Domains

As we saw earlier, top-level members are called domains. It is common and recommended practice to only have one domain per dimension, in other words, to not have more than one member report element below a dimension report element. Semantically, this is a special member report element that represents the overall (aggregated) value across the entire domain of members below it. This is the reason why it is also called domain, i.e., we identify this top-level member with the set of all its descendants from a semantic perspective.

In the example at hand, the domain associated with the director dimension allows provides a value for each concept (salary, bonus, and so on) aggregated across all directors in the company.

While it would be allowed by XBRL, we discourage any other use of the top-level member report element. In particular, it is not advisable to pick a random member and place it at the top of the hierarchy.

7.3.2   Member arrangement patterns

There are several ways that the hierarchy of members can be aggregated. Charles Hofmann investigated reports submitted to the EDGAR system, and distinguished the following types of member hierarchies:

- whole-part hierarchies. In a whole-part hierarchy, the values associated with child members actually add up to the value associated with the parent member, in a way similar to roll-ups for concepts. This works recursively, meaning that a child member can itself contain further child members that add up to it.

- is-a hierarchies. In an is-a hierarchy, the values do not necessarily add up. This means that, while child members semantically represent a subdomain of the parent member, the list of members may not be comprehensive. This also works recursively, meaning that a child member can itself contain further child members representing subdomains or leaves.

In the director compensation example, the director dimension is using a whole-part hierarchy: for each concept, the value associated with the domain (all directors) is the sum of the value associated with John Doe and Jane Doe.

The semantics of whole-part hierarchies can be enforced using formulas, just like the semantics of roll-ups are enforced with calculation networks. Formulas are covered with an extensive set of XBRL specification that deserves a chapter of their own, so we also leave this aside and assume for the moment that the burden is on the creator of the instance to check that values add up correctly in whole-part hierarchies.

Again, we insist that, while XBRL theoretically allows doing so, it is unadvised to build hierarchies of members in any other way than the above two member arrangement patterns.

7.4 Default dimension members

XBRL supports defining a default member for each explicit dimension. Within a DTS, a dimension may only contain a single default member that is in force across all the DTS.

Aspect	Characteristic
Concept	Director, Salary
Entity	Sample Company
Period	January 1, 2017 to December 31, 2017
Unit	U.S. Dollars
Fact value	1,000

Figure 7.15: A fact that does not carry the Director dimension, and thus implicitly associates this dimension with its default member (all directors).

The semantics of default members is that, in an XBRL instance, a fact that is reported with this default member MUST omit this dimension and member in its list of associated characteristics[12]. What happens is that, if one needs to display a hypercube with a certain number of dimensions, for example according to a presentation network, facts that do not use one or several of these dimensions will still appear on the rendering, and the default member will be automatically added on the logical level.

In our example with the director compensation network, the default member of the director dimension is the domain member (all directors). This means that the facts with this domain member, i.e. the last four facts on Figure 7.4, carry this default member with them on the logical level, but not on the physical level. This can be seen looking at a single fact representation, shown on Figure 7.15: the director dimension is absent.

In particular, these facts also appear in a fact table with the director dimension removed, as shown on Figure 7.16. Semanti-

---

[12]For the observing reader, this means that the domain `us-gaap:Income StatementLocationDomain` shown on Figure 7.3 does not actually physically appear in the fact, because it happens to be the default member of `us-gaap: IncomeStatementLocationAxis`.

Concept	Entity	Period	Unit	Value
Directory, Salary	Sample Company	January 1, 2017 thru December 31, 2017	U.S. Dollars	2,000
Directory, Bonus	Sample Company	January 1, 2017 thru December 31, 2017	U.S. Dollars	2,000
Directory, Fee	Sample Company	January 1, 2017 thru December 31, 2017	U.S. Dollars	2,000
Directory, Options Granted, at Fair Value	Sample Company	January 1, 2017 thru December 31, 2017	U.S. Dollars	2,000

Figure 7.16: The fact table corresponding to the hypercube of director compensation, but with the director dimension removed. Only those facts that implicitly use the default member of the director dimension are thus shown, so that only aggregated values can be seen.

cally, this is a roll-up, i.e., we are zooming out, looking only at the aggregated value across the entire domain of this dimension.

XBRL forbids explicit use of default members, meaning that it is an error to store a fact in an XBRL instance that associates a dimension with its default member as defined in the associated DTS.

It is common, and recommended practice, to use the domain as the default member of a dimension. While XBRL would allow picking a random member and set it as default, doing so will bring a lot of issues and unexpected behavior when displaying renderings. The default member must coincide with the whole domain of the dimension for this to make sense. In other word, facts omitting dimensions automatically report a value that is the aggregate value over the entire dimension domain.

Default members are central to the dimensional semantics of XBRL: indeed, this means that a fact omitting a dimension can appear in a hypercube that does not have this dimension, but also in a hypercube that has this dimension if it has a default member. In the latter case, this fact will appear along with facts that specify values for other members. This is very convenient for analysts to navigate through hypercubes rolling up dimensional hierarchies.

Note that, even though we are talking about default members in this section because this is relevant for user-friendly display, they are not defined in presentation networks. Default members are defined in definition networks as explained in Section 7.6.

7.5   Networks with multiple hypercubes

Figure 7.17 shows a hypothetical presentation network that contains three hypercubes, taken from our existing examples. The corresponding network thus has three components. Furthermore, in this example, for the sake of generality, one of the three hypercubes is implicit.

Figures 7.18, 7.19 and 7.20 shows the three component renderings. Note how they are built separately from each other.

99999 - Some Big Network With Three Components

Report element	Kind	Type	Balance	Period Type
Accounting policies, PPE and Director Compensation [Abstract]	Abstract	-	-	-
Accounting policies [Hierarchy]	Abstract	-	-	-
Basis of presentation	Concept	Text block	instant	-
Trade receivables policy	Concept	Text block	instant	-
Inventory policies [Abstract]	Abstract	-	-	-
Inventory valuation method	Concept	Text block	-	instant
Description of inventory components	Concept	Text block	-	instant
Inventory cost method	Concept	Text block	-	instant
Investments in securities policy	Concept	Text block	-	instant
Bank borrowing policy	Concept	Text block	-	instant
Provisions policy	Concept	Text block	-	instant
Property, plant and equipment [Table]	Hypercube	-	-	-
Property, plant and equipment [Line Items]	LineItems	-	-	-
Property, plant and equipment [Roll Up]	Abstract	-	-	-
Land	Concept	Monetary	debit	instant
Buildings, net	Concept	Monetary	debit	instant
Furniture and fixtures, net	Concept	Monetary	debit	instant
Computer equipment, net	Concept	Monetary	debit	instant
Other property, plant and equipment, net	Concept	Monetary	debit	instant
Property, plant and equipment, net	Concept	Monetary	debit	instant
Director Compensation [Table]	Hypercube	-	-	-
Director [Axis]	Dimension	-	-	-
All directors [Domain]	Member	-	*	-
John Doe [Member]	Member	-	-	-
Jane Doe [Member]	Member	-	-	-
Director Compensation [Line Items]	LineItems	-	-	-
Director Compensation [Hierarchy]	Abstract	-	-	-
Director, Salary	Concept	Monetary	credit	instant
Director, Bonus	Concept	Monetary	credit	instant
Director, Fee	Concept	Monetary	credit	instant
Director, Options Granted, at Fair Value	Concept	Monetary	credit	instant

Figure 7.17: The presentation network of a network with three components, one of which implicit. The explicit components correspond to the subtrees below the hypercube report elements (depth 1). The implicit component corresponds to everything else, that is, the presentation network with hypercubes and their subtrees removed, that is, the accounting policies hierarchy. The top-level abstract has no semantic significance.

Network	99999 - Some Big Network With Three Components
Hypercube	Implied Table [Table]

Entity [Axis]	Sample Company
Period [Axis]	Jan. 1 to Dec. 31st, 2010
Language [Axis]	U.S. English

Accounting policies [Line Items]	
Accounting policies [Hierarchy]	
Basis of presentation	Praesent fringilla feugiat magna. Suspendisse et lorem eu risus convallis placerat.Suspendisse potenti. Donec malesuada loremid mi. Nunc ut purus ac nisl tempus accumsan.
Trade receivables policy	Sed magna felis, accumsan a, fermentum quis, varius sed, ipsum. Nullam leo. Donec eros.
Inventory policies [Abstract]	
Inventory valuation method	Cost
Description of inventory components	Proin elit sem, ornare non, ullamcorper vel, sollicitudin a, lacus. Mauris tincidunt cursus est. Nulla sit amet nibh. Sed elementum feugiat augue. Nam
Inventory cost method	FIFO
Investments in securities policy	Etiam ipsum orci, gravida nec, feugiat ut, malesuada quis, mauris. Etiam porttitor. Ut venenatis, velit a accumsan interdum, odio metus mollis mauris, non pharetra augue arcu eu felis.
Bank borrowing policy	Ut ut risus nec nibh dictum posuere. Phasellus eleifend, diam vitae dapibus pulvinar, erat ligula auctor dui, eget conguejusto lorem hendrerit tellus.
Provisions policy	vestibulum augue eu justo. Pellentesque habitant morbi tristique senectus et netus et malesuada fames ac turpis egestas.

Figure 7.18: Possible renderings of each one of the three components of the big network: 1. The implicit component (implied table)

Network	99999 - Some Big Network With Three Components	
Hypercube	Property, plant and equipment [Table]	

Entity [Axis]	Sample Company	
Unit [Axis]	U.S. Dollars	

	Period [Axis]	
Property, plant and equipment [Line Items]	Jan. 1 to Dec. 31st, 2009	Jan. 1 to Dec. 31st, 2010
Property, plant and equipment [Roll Up]		
Land	1,147,000	5,347,000
Buildings, net	366,375,000	244,508,000
Furniture and fixtures, net	34,457,000	34,457,000
Computer equipment, net	5,313,000	4,169,000
Other property, plant and equipment, net	6,149,000	6,702,000
Property, plant and equipment, net	413,441,000	295,183,000

Figure 7.19: Possible renderings of each one of the three components of the big network: 2. The first explicit component.

Network	99999 - Some Big Network With Three Components		
Hypercube	Director Compensation [Table]		

Entity [Axis]	Sample Company		
Period [Axis]	Jan. 1 to Dec. 31st, 2010		
Unit [Axis]	U.S. Dollars		

	Director [Axis]		
	All directors [Domain]		
Director Compensation [Line Items]	John Doe [Member]	Jane Doe [Member]	
Director Compensation [Hierarchy]			
Director, Salary	1,000	1,000	2,000
Director, Bonus	1,000	1,000	2,000
Director, Fee	1,000	1,000	2,000
Director, Options Granted, at Fair Value	1,000	1,000	2,000

Figure 7.20: Possible renderings of each one of the three components of the big network: 3. The second explicit component.

7.6   Definition networks

7.6.1   Hypercube validation

Until now, we have extended presentation networks with hypercubes, dimensions, members and line-item report elements. This allowed us to group facts in cubes and display them nicely in components, themselves grouped in networks.

All a presentation network does is carry information regarding how to display components to the end user. It is important to know that presentation networks do not perform any validation. Their purpose is not to restrict the usage of certain dimensions with a given concept, or the usage of certain members with a given dimension. If the instance contains a fact that has more dimensions that those in the presentation network, or that associates a dimension with a member not present below it in the presentation network, nobody will complain about this.

Instead, this kind of validation is done by means of a definition network. Like for presentation networks, a definition network is a subset of an entire definition linkbase, and that subset is identified with a network identifier. In presentation-based reports, the definition network, calculation network and presentation network that share the same network identifier belong together and, together, make up this network: the definition network takes care of hypercube(s) validity, the calculation network takes care of concept summation validity, and the presentation network takes care of hinting at how to display the network properly.

The definition network is optional, but should always be present when using dimensions to make sure that the reported facts are consistent and meaningful. Networks with no hypercubes besides the implicit table may also contain a (trivial) definition network that associates all concepts with a dimensionless hypercube. For DPM-based taxonomies, it plays a paramount role.

7.6.2 How definition networks look like

Definition networks are similar to presentation networks and calculation networks, in that they are DAGs of report elements[13]. These definition network DAGs specify:

1. to which hypercube(s) a concept belongs (more precisely: to which components, as we saw that hypercube names alone can be ambiguous).

2. with which dimensions a hypercube is associated (within the current network, that is, for the corresponding component).

3. which members belong to each dimension (within the current component).

4. which member is the default member (if any) of each dimension (across the entire DTS).

As can be seen in the above list, definition networks do not specify how facts are to be displayed: they specify whether facts are valid or not.

Figures 7.21 gives an example of definition network. Note how, while it is similar to a presentation network, the line-items and hypercube report elements are swapped, in that the hypercube report element is a child of the line-items report element in a definition network.

The Director Compensation [Table] hypercube is associated with the Director [Axis] dimension, and below that dimension is the hierarchy of all its members. In particular, All directors [Domain], John Doe [Member] and Jane Doe [Member] are the three members that belong to the domain of the Director [Axis], with the top-level member embodying this domain.

---

[13]It is common practice to enforce that these should be trees, that is, with no undirected cycles

50000 - Director Compensation

Report element	Kind	Default
Director Compensation [Line Items]	LineItems	-
Director Compensation [Table]	Hypercube	-
Director [Axis]	Dimension	All directors [Domain]
All directors [Domain]	Member	-
John Doe [Member]	Member	-
Jane Doe [Member]	Member	-
Director Compensation [Hierarchy]	Abstract	-
Director, Salary	Concept	-
Director, Bonus	Concept	-
Director, Fee	Concept	-
Director, Options Granted, at Fair Value	Concept	-

Figure 7.21: A definition network corresponding to our previous example of director compensation (we use standard labels). Note that definition networks typically do not have the top-level abstracts.

7.6.3   Relating facts to definition networks

The Director Compensation [Line Items] line-items report element is associated with this hypercube, and by transitivity, so are all its descendants Director Compensation [Hierarchy], Director, Salary, Director, Bonus, Director, Fee and Director, Options Granted, at Fair Value.

Concretely, this means that the definition network allows reporting facts against one of the above concepts, say, the Director, Salary concept, with these facts having a dimension Director [Axis], and acceptable members associated with this dimension are All directors [Domain], John Doe [Member] and Jane Doe [Member].

Furthermore, the dimension Director [Axis] has the default member All directors [Domain], meaning that this aggregated-domain value is implicit for facts that do not use the Director [Axis] dimension, and that it is even forbidden to even use it explicitly alongside Director [Axis].

Figure 7.22 shows a few facts that are valid against the Director Compensation [Table] hypercube and in the current network, according to the above explanations.

Aspect	Characteristic
Concept	Director, Salary
Entity	Sample Company
Period	January 1, 2017 to December 31, 2017
Unit	U.S. Dollars
Director [Axis]	Jane Doe [Member]
Fact value	1,000

(a) A valid fact, using the Jane Doe [Member]

Aspect	Characteristic
Concept	Director, Fee
Entity	Sample Company
Period	January 1, 2017 to December 31, 2017
Unit	U.S. Dollars
Director [Axis]	John Doe [Member]
Fact value	3,000

(b) A valid fact, using the John Doe [Member]

Aspect	Characteristic
Concept	Director, Bonus
Entity	Sample Company
Period	January 1, 2017 to December 31, 2017
Unit	U.S. Dollars
Fact value	2,000

(c) A valid fact, using the All Directors [Domain] member. This must be implicit because it is the default member.

Figure 7.22: A few facts valid against the previously defined definition network.

Figure 7.23 shows a few facts that are not valid according to the above explanations. Note that some of these facts may become valid if one extends the DTS with appropriate, new definition networks, thus creating new allowed cubes, or modifies the existing ones.

Aspect	Characteristic
Concept	Director, Salary
Entity	Sample Company
Period	January 1, 2017 to December 31, 2017
Unit	U.S. Dollars
Director [Axis]	Bill Doe [Member]
Fact value	1,000

(a) An invalid fact, using the Bill Doe [Member] which, while it may exist in the taxonomy, does not appear below the Director [Axis] dimension in the definition network.

Aspect	Characteristic
Concept	Director, Vacations left
Entity	Sample Company
Period	January 1, 2017 to December 31, 2017
Unit	decimal
Director [Axis]	John Doe [Member]
Fact value	10.2

(b) An invalid fact, using the Director, Vacations left concept which, while it may exist in the taxonomy, does not appear in the transitive closure of the Director Compensation [Line Items] report element, and thus does not belong to the component.

Aspect	Characteristic
Concept	Director, Bonus
Entity	Sample Company
Period	January 1, 2017 to December 31, 2017
Unit	U.S. Dollars
Director [Axis]	All Directors [Domain]
Fact value	2,000

(c) An invalid fact, using the All Directors [Domain] member explicitly although it is the default member.

Figure 7.23: A few facts that are not valid against the previously defined definition network.

30000 - Property, Plant, and Equipment, by Component		
Report element	Kind	Default
Property, plant and equipment [Line Items]	LineItems	-
Property, plant and equipment [Table]	Hypercube	-
Property, plant and equipment [Roll Up]	Abstract	-
Land	Concept	-
Buildings, net	Concept	-
Furniture and fixtures, net	Concept	-
Computer equipment, net	Concept	-
Other property, plant and equipment, net	Concept	-
Property, plant and equipment, net	Concept	-

Figure 7.24: A definition network corresponding to our previous example of property, plant and equipment, with a hypercube that has no dimensions.

Finally, Figure 7.24 shows a trivial definition network with no dimension. If this hypercube is closed[14], this forbids usage of any dimensions in facts that use concepts from this hierarchy.

---

[14]we will see what this means later

7.6.4   Consistency of a definition network

A definition network has a few consistency constraints, most of which are ensure at the syntactic level of XBRL.

Edges can only go:

- From a hypercube to a dimension. These are called *hypercube-dimension* edges.

- From a dimension to a member. These are called *dimension-member* edges.

- From a concept, abstract or line-items report element to a hypercube. These are called *all* edges. Best practice dictates that it should actually only be from a line-items report element to a hypercube. We will see that there are also *notAll* edges for negating a hypercube. These edges, positive or negative are also collectively referred to as *has-hypercube* edges.

- From a member to a member. These are called *domain-member* edges.

- From a concept, abstract or line-items report element to a concept or abstract report element. These are also called *domain-member* edges (for some obscure reason that we will not go into[15]). Best practice dictates that concepts should normally only be at the leaves.

---

[15]The XBRL syntax technically does not disallow mixing members with concept, abstract and line-items report elements using *domain-member* edges. This is because no distinction is made on the syntactic level between abstracts and members. We cannot emphasize enough, though, how this distinction is crucial for a clean taxonomy, and how it is important to separate the member hierarchies from the line-items-concept-abstract hierarchies.

50000 - Director Compensation		
Report element	Kind	Arc role
Director Compensation [Line Items]	LineItems	-
Director Compensation [Table]	Hypercube	all
Director [Axis]	Dimension	hypercube-dimension
All directors [Domain]	Member	dimension-domain
John Doe [Member]	Member	domain-member
Jane Doe [Member]	Member	domain-member
Director Compensation [Hierarchy]	Abstract	domain-member
Director, Salary	Concept	domain-member
Director, Bonus	Concept	domain-member
Director, Fee	Concept	domain-member
Director, Options Granted, at Fair Value	Concept	domain-member

Figure 7.25: A definition network where we explicitly give the arc roles of the edges (every time: to the current row from the direct parent).

Figure 7.25 shows the previous definition network, where we explicitly show what kind of edges connect the various report elements. These kinds of edges are called arc roles[16].

7.6.5   A more formal explanation of hypercube validation

The examples in the previous section should be enough to understand the general idea. For completeness, we also give a more formal explanation. In this section, we first only consider positive open hypercubes for simplicity. We will tackle negative hypercubes as well as closed and open hypercubes later.

---

[16]The arc role is actually a longer URI, as we will see in the syntax section. This is all standardized.

Validity of a fact against a single network

To test validity of a fact reported against a concept C in a given network N, we must find the hypercubes H in that network that are relevant to C. In order to do this, we consider the list of all report elements that are ancestors of C in the DAG obtained with *domain-member* edges, in other words, the transitive closure navigating the directed domain-member edges backwards. Then we look for all hypercubes bound via an *all* edge to at least one of these report elements. These are the relevant hypercubes for C.

A fact is valid against the network N if it is valid against all the relevant hypercubes. Validity against a network is thus the conjunction of validity against the individual, relevant hypercubes. If the fact is not valid against even just one of these hypercubes, then validity against the network fails.

If there are no hypercubes relevant to the reported concept in the network, then validity is irrelevant, but for pedagogical reasons we can say that in such cases, the fact is invalid against the network if no hypercube is relevant, i.e., the fact belongs to no hypercube in this network.

Validity of a fact against a single hypercube (within a network)

Let us assume we are looking at a network N, and let us look closer at a single hypercube H that is relevant for the concept C considered.

A fact is valid against hypercube H if the following holds: whenever the fact uses a dimension D that appears below H in the network N, the member M that the fact associates with D[17,18], must

---

[17]This can also be implicit if D's default member is M and and D is not explicitly in the fact's aspects. In this case, the default member is assumed to be associated with D.

[18]If D is explicitly associated with its default member, the fact is invalid,

be in the transitive closure of D (its domain) in network N.

In other words, if a fact associates a dimension with a member (implicitly or explicitly), and the hypercube has that dimension, and the member does not appear in the dimension's member hierarchy, then the fact is invalid against that hypercube.

Validity of a fact that uses dimensions beyond those defined in the hypercube depends on whether the hypercube is closed or open, which we will see shortly.

Overall validity of a fact (against the whole DTS)

A fact is, in terms of dimensionality, valid against the DTS if we find at least one network against which the fact is valid with the above definition, or if the concept of the fact is not associated with any hypercube in any network[19]. In other words, validation across networks is disjunctive, while validation across hypercubes within a network is conjunctive.

Note how, in XBRL, the universal (inside a network) and existential (across networks) quantifications do not naturally extend to the empty set, which may disturb mathematical minds. If the set of relevant hypercubes is empty, then the "universal quantifier" on these non-existent hypercubes returns false [20]. If the set of relevant networks is empty, then the "existential quantifier" on these non-existent networks returns true [21].

7.6.6 Open and closed hypercubes

XBRL allows for hypercubes to be open or closed.

---

but it is invalid with respect to the semantics of dimensions in general, not with respect to this specific hypercube.

[19]The absence of a definition linkbase thus places no hypercube validation constraints.

[20]I can here mathematicians say "ouch!" from here

[21]Double-"ouch!"

If, given a network, a hypercube associated with a set of concepts is closed, and a fact is reported against one of these concepts, then validity against this hypercube is strengthened with an additional condition: this fact must not carry any dimension that is not in this hypercube. If the hypercube is open, this constraint is waived. Thus, if a hypercube is marked as open, then a fact with dimensions not belonging to that hypercube will still be valid against that hypercube no matter which members it associates to them[22].

It is common practice to close hypercubes.

7.6.7   Consistency between definition and presentation networks

Definition networks and presentation networks have orthogonal duties: the former validates data, while the latter specifies how to display it to the end user.

We previously mentioned that they are similar, not only because they are both DAGs of report elements, but also because in the realm of presentation-based reports, it is best practice, in each network, to keep the definition network and the presentation network consistent with each other[23]. It is only logical that the data is presented in a way that matches its internal structure, including its consistency. This only applies to presentation-based taxonomies, as DPM-based taxonomies do not rely on presentation networks for displaying components.

- A *hypercube-dimension* edge in the definition network should correspond 1 to 1 to an edge going from the same hypercube to the same dimension in the presentation network.

---

[22]As long as it does not explicitly associates the default member of that dimension, which is incorrect XBRL

[23]In DPM-based reports, the definition network is consistent with the table linkbase rather than the presentation linkbase.

- A *dimension-member* edge in the definition network should correspond 1 to 1 to an edge going from the same dimension to the same member in the presentation network.

- A *domain-member* edge binding a member with a member in the definition network should correspond 1 to 1 to an edge going from the same outbound member to the same inbound member in the presentation network.

- A *domain-member* edge binding a line-items/abstract/concept with an abstract/concept in the definition network should correspond 1 to 1 to an edge going from the same outbound report element to the same inbound report element in the presentation network.

- An *all* edge binding a line-items report element with a hypercube in the definition network should correspond 1 to 1 to an edge going from the hypercube to the line-items report element (mind the swap of direction) in the presentation network[24].

The above criteria put restrictions on presentation networks compared to what XBRL allows, that is, any report element could in theory be bound with any other report element in presentation, however it is common practice to restrict presentation networks in such a way, and many taxonomies worldwide, those that are not DPM-based, are following the EDGAR guidelines. It is also advisable to do so when designing new presentation-based taxonomies.

See for example the consistency between the presentation network shown on Figure 7.11, and the definition network shown on Figure 7.21.

---

[24]It should be mentioned that some taxonomies, such as in Japan, treat this differently, and have the hypercube and line-items report element appear as siblings in the presentation network, below the top-level abstract. This design implies that all hypercube in a network must share the same hierarchies of line-items, concepts and abstracts.

7.6.8 Negative hypercubes

XBRL also allows for defining negative hypercubes. A negative
hypercube looks like a normal hypercube, but the difference is that
it is bound to the report element hierarchy with a *notAll* edge
instead of an *all* edge[25].

The semantics of a negative hypercube for the validation of a
fact against a network is as defined in Section 7.6.5, except that
validity is negated: a fact is valid against the negative hypercube
if it would have been invalid, had that hypercube been positive. A
fact is thus valid against a negative hypercube if it associates at
least one dimension with a member that is not in the domain of
that dimension.

A typical usecase for negative hypercubes is to appear jointly
with a bigger positive hypercube in a network: remember the conjunction semantics of validation within a network. The negative
hypercubes thus mark some regions of the positive hypercube as
forbidden.

Usage of negative hypercubes is discouraged in presentation-
based taxonomies, where each network should contain as many
positive hypercubes as appear in the presentation network.

Usage of negative hypercubes is also fully avoided in DPM-
based taxonomies, which prefer additive hypercubes. In DPM-
based taxonomies, additive hypercubes are obtained by spreading
them over multiple networks[26], which allows validity to be achieved
by disjunction of individual positive hypercube validity rather than
by conjunction of a big positive hypercube with a few negative
hypercubes.

---

[25]It has the implication that a hypercube could be positive for some report
element and network, and negative for another report element and network

[26]Recall that if the same network contains several hypercubes, facts that
use a concept present in several of them must be valid against all the relevant
hypercubes (conjunction)

A hypercube can also be both closed and negative. In this case, a fact can also be valid against a negative, closed hypercube if it uses extra dimensions.

Furthermore, the Edgar Filing Manual (SEC) forbids closed negative hypercubes and advises using open positive hypercubes instead.

7.6.9 Modular definition networks

XBRL allows modularity and reusability in definition networks. This feature is mostly used in DPM-based taxonomies and is discouraged in presentation-based taxonomies.

A modular definition network may have its DAG edges spread over multiple other networks, as follows.

A modular definition network contains *all* and *notAll* edges binding a report element to a hypercube, like what we have seen until now. These edges are the starting point. However, modularity is achieved in that these edges may carry a stamp that indicates that the *hypercube-dimension* edges that point to the dimensions of that hypercube are in a *different* network. This is called a target network[27]. This means that several networks can reuse and share dimension definitions, which saves space.

The same applies to any kind of edge: a *hypercube-dimension* edge can also carry a stamp indicating that the *dimension-domain* edges are to be found in yet another network. This allows the reuse of dimension domains.

Likewise, a *dimension-domain* edge can also carry a stamp indicating that the *domain-member* edges are to be found in yet another network. And finally, and recursively, a *domain-member* can also carry a stamp indicating that the next *domain-member* edges (that is, the next level of the hierarchy) are to be found in

---

[27]targetRole on the syntactic level

yet another network. This allows reusing member hierarchies as well as line-items/abstract/concept hierarchies.

Looking at modular definition networks with a logical perspective

The best way to look at modular definition networks is to distinguish between a logical level and a physical level. The above stamps, and the distribution of edges across different networks should be seen as a physical implementation. From a logical perspective, starting with the *all* and *notAll* edges in a network N, one navigates down the edges, following the stamp indications that may lead to other networks, and one obtains a resulting DAG. This DAG should be seen as the logical DAG of the network N. It is irrelevant, on the logical level, that this DAG was obtained with edges from different networks. From a logical perspective, it is *as if* the entire DAG had physically had all its edges in network N.

Not that, in a modular definition network, not all edges must carry such stamps. Some may, some others may not. In the absence of stamps, navigation down the DAG remains in the same current network.

Figure 7.26 shows an example of the physical level of a few modular networks, sharing some structure.

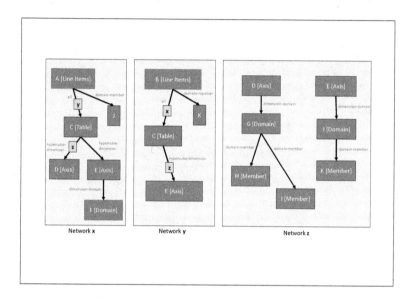

Figure 7.26: A modular set of definition networks (x, y and z). Some edges have a target role, which is a network identifier (also x, y or z) that says where to continue resolving edges to build the logical definition networks. For simplicity, we kept hierarchies simple. Arc roles appear in gray, even though they would be clear anyway as report element kinds are marked in square brackets.

Figure 7.27 shows how this maps to logical DAG structures. In practice, only this logical structure matters. The physical structure only matters when parsing the definition linkbase and building these logical DAGs.

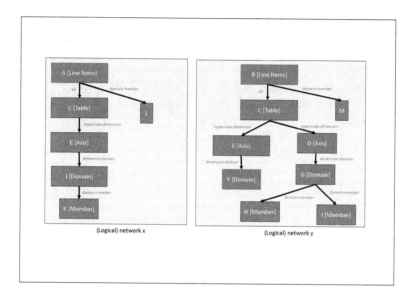

Figure 7.27: The logical definition networks that should be exposed to the user, after resolving the target roles from the physical definition networks. If one looks at network x from the point of view of the end user, any concepts below line-items report element A are associated with a hypercube C that only has the E axis. This is because A was physically pointing to C with a target role y, so that the corresponding axes were resolved in the physical network y rather than x. Likewise, the domain hierarchy of axis E was resolved in the physical network z, because C was physically pointing to E with a target role z.

DPM-Taxonomy designers vs. XBRL report consumers and analysts

XBRL end users should only be exposed to the physical level of a modular definition network if they have to decide how to share and reuse definition structures, for example, hierarchies of members or hierarchies of report elements, and how to save space. This is the case for taxonomy designers. Consumers of XBRL data, however, should be fully shielded from this mechanism as it is fully irrelevant to them.

7.7 Summary of naming conventions

As we saw in this chapter, many taxonomies follow US GAAP principles and use "table" as a synonym for "hypercube", "axis" as a synonym for "dimension", "domain" as a synonym for "top-level member", "line-items" as a synonym for top-level abstract. XBRL users should be familiar with these conventions and have an open mind regarding this terminology.

The word "concept" is sometimes used (including in the XBRL specifications) as a generic term for all report elements, but we recommend avoiding using it in this way. Use only "concept" for non-abstract items, i.e., actually reportable concepts, but be aware that you may find this alternate meaning in some architectural documents.

The word "base set" is sometimes used as a terminology for a given presentation network, definition network (sometimes restricted to specific arc roles) or calculation network. We recommend avoiding this terminology altogether at the user level, because "base set" is more of a physical, implementation detail than an actual part of the XBRL data model. Prefer the use of the words "taxonomy linkbase", "network" (across all kinds of linkbases), "component" (for a specific pair of network and hypercube), "presentation linkbase" (across all networks), a specific "presentation network", "label linkbase" (rarely a specific network), "calculation linkbase", a specific "calculation network", "definition linkbase", a specific "definition network", and within this definition network, hierarchies of report elements (members, or line items).

7.8 Summary of best practices

We now summarize the best practices that we recommended in this chapter. The credits for some of those go to the EDGAR Filer Manual, some others to Charles Hoffman who did extensive research on common practices in EDGAR filings and issued his recommendations. The first list applies to both presentation-based taxonomies and DPM-based taxonomies:

1. Do not use implicit hypercubes (implied tables).

2. Clearly classify report elements as belonging to one of the six kinds and give them appropriate internal names (conventions vary between presentation-based and DPM-based) and, for presentation-based taxonomies, labels (kinds in square brackets).

3. For any hypercube, associate a dimension with only one domain (top-level member).

4. Always organize member hierarchies in one of the two semantically meaningful ways, and document it so: whole-part or is-a.

5. Always choose the top-level domain as the default member of a dimension.

6. Avoid negative hypercubes in general.

7. Avoid open hypercubes in general.

This second list applies to presentation-based taxonomies:

1. Use different hypercube report elements across networks. Do not use the same hypercube in different networks.

2. Only use one hypercube per network, i.e., networks should only have each one component.

3. Avoid typed dimensions when you can.

4. Keep presentation, definition and calculation linkbases consistent.

5. Avoid using modular definition networks, unless you have a good reason, such as avoiding redundant storage of hierarchies.

Be aware that not all taxonomies designed to date and not all reports filed to date follow these best practices, so it is important to have the knowledge and flexibility to also understand reports that use different conventions, because they are also correct XBRL. Charles Hoffman noted on occasion that the term "common practice" may be more accurate to name these recommendations than "best practice". We expect that in the future, as XBRL acceptance increases, these practices may converge.

7.9 How not to handle dimensionality

In the early days of XBRL, before the dimensions specification was published, dimensionality was handled in different ways, mainly two. We detail them here for historical reasons, and because it is important to be able to understand older reports, however, it is discouraged to use these mechanisms in new taxonomies. Hypercubes, dimensions and definition networks are the correct way of building cubes of data in XBRL.

7.9.1 Tuples

Until now, we only looked at facts reporting atomic values. In this and former chapters, we saw how to structure and show these facts together in various ways thanks to presentation and definition networks.

In the core XBRL specification, which was published before dimensions were introduced, another way is given to build structured facts. This is done by means of complex XML Schema elements. Facts, instead of being listed standalone as a flat list in the instance, can also be grouped in tuples, themselves in other tuples, and so

220 CHAPTER 7. HYPERCUBES

on. A fact thus has meaning within the tuples that it belongs too and not only according to its context. In other words, the parent tuples contribute to the context of the fact as well, in addition to the concept, period, entity, unit and language.

It is recommended not to use tuples, because:

- Tuples expose the XML data model explicitly, which is not desirable according to the data independence paradigm. In XBRL, tree structures involving report elements should be exposed via linkbases and not via XML complex types.

- In the aspect model, tuples also involve XPath expressions, which should also not be exposed to the end user as XML and XPath belong to the syntactic level, not to the actual data model of XBRL.

- XBRL dimensions provide a better way to structure facts, using data cubes semantics that seamlessly extends the five builtin aspects.

7.9.2 Syntactic segments and scenarios

The XBRL core specification allows extra, free XML complex content as part of the context of the facts, in so-called segment and scenario containers. This is again a purely syntactic feature that the end user should not know of because it exposes XML-specific content.

The XBRL dimensions specification makes use of this feature, but it hides and encapsulates it, and all the user sees is what we explained in this chapter. As we will see in the next section, the free XML complex content in scenario and segment containers is actually used to store all the members (or typed values) associated with various dimensions for a fact, but this is completely hidden from the users.

It is best practice to not use segment and scenario containers in any other way than specified in the following section explain the XML syntax of dimensional facts, and to not bother the user with these details.

7.10 XML Syntax of definition networks

Now that we have seen how users can extend hypercubes with their own dimensions on top of the five builtin aspects, we take a look at the XML syntax with which the new four report elements can be declared, as well as definition networks.

Again, we cannot emphasize enough how important it is to separate the XBRL data model from the XML syntax that now follows. This concept of data independence dates back to 1970 and is even more crucial for definition networks than for everything we saw in previous chapters. Learning about hypercube validation and definition networks by the means of XML syntax is a sure way to convince oneself that this is very complicated. It is not, as much of the complexity comes from the syntactic layer and should be hidden from end users.

7.10.1 Declaration of the new report elements

New namespace bindings

Hypercube validation machinery and user-defined aspects are introduced in the XBRL Dimensions 1.0 specification. Two namespaces are introduced:

- `http://xbrl.org/2005/xbrldt`, associated with the `xbrldt`, used in taxonomies.

- `http://xbrl.org/2005/xbrldi`, associated with the `xbrldi`, used in instances.

```
<xs:element
     xmlns:xs="http://www.w3.org/2001/XMLSchema"
     xmlns:xbrli="http://www.xbrl.org/2003/instance"
     xmlns:xbrldt="http://xbrl.org/2005/xbrldt"
     name="StatementTable"                Hypercube metadata
     substitutionGroup="xbrldt:hypercubeItem"
     abstract="true"
     xbrli:periodType="duration"
     type="xbrli:stringItemType"
     nillable="true"/>
```

Figure 7.28: A report element declaration which defines the hypercube us-gaap:StatementTable. It appears in an XBRL taxonomy schema. We include the prefix bindings, although in practice they are on the root xbrli:xbrl element

Hypercube report elements

A hypercube is declared with a syntax very similar to that for concepts and abstracts. Figure 7.28 shows the syntax for declaring a hypercube.

What characterizes the report element as a hypercube is that its substitution group is xbrldt:hypercubeItem, and it must be abstract. The **name** attribute carries the local name of the declared hypercube.

The other attributes are purely syntactic and have either mandatory values, or best practice values:

- the **nillable** attribute should be set to true.

- the **type** attribute should be set to xbrli:stringItemType.

- the xbrli:periodType attribute should be set to duration.

```
<xs:element
    xmlns:xs="http://www.w3.org/2001/XMLSchema"
    xmlns:xbrli="http://www.xbrl.org/2003/instance"
    xmlns:xbrldt="http://xbrl.org/2005/xbrldt"

    name="AircraftTypeAxis"           Dimension metadata
    substitutionGroup="xbrldt:dimensionItem"
    abstract="true"

    xbrli:periodType="duration"
    type="xbrli:stringItemType"
    nillable="true"/>
```

Figure 7.29: A report element declaration which defines the dimension **us-gaap:AircraftTypeAxis**. It appears in an XBRL taxonomy schema. We include the prefix bindings, although in practice they are on the root **xbrli:xbrl** element

The last three attributes have no effect, as hypercubes cannot be nilled, have no types and no period types. They are here for modular reasons, as the dimensions specification was introduced later than the core XBRL 2.1 specification.

Dimension report elements

A dimension is declared with a syntax very similar to that for concepts and abstracts as well. Figure 7.29 shows the syntax for declaring an explicit dimension.

What characterizes the report element as a dimension is that its substitution group is **xbrldt:dimensionItem**, and it must be abstract. The **name** attribute carries the local name of the declared dimension.

The other attributes are purely syntactic and have either mandatory values, or best practice values:

- the `nillable` attribute should be set to true.

- the `type` attribute should be set to `xbrli:stringItemType`. This syntactic report element type has nothing to do with the type of a typed dimension. The dimension may well be a typed dimension with an integer, or date value space, and still carry `xbrli:stringItemType` as its report element type. This must be hidden from the end user.

- the `xbrli:periodType` attribute should be set to `duration`.

These attributes have no effect, as dimensions cannot be nilled, have no types and no period types. They are here for modular reasons, as the dimensions specification was introduced later than the core XBRL 2.1 specification.

A typed dimension looks the same, but has an an additional attribute `xbrldt:typedDomainRef`, which points to an element declaration.

Figure 7.30 shows an example of how a typed dimension can be declared, in this case with an integer type.

The syntactic value associated with that type dimension in the instance must be an element that matches this element declaration. It is best practice to stick to elements that have a simple type, such as string, integer, dateTime. That simple type is then, from a data modelling perspective, the type of the typed dimension as described earlier in this chapter.

The element declaration may be in a different schema, or in the same (taxonomy) schema. The syntax of the URI to reference this element declaration (XPointer) is the same as that used by linkbases to reference XBRL report elements.

While XBRL allows typed dimensions with any complex type, this is not recommended, because it would force the exposition of

```
<xs:schema
    xmlns:xs="http://www.w3.org/2001/XMLSchema"
    targetNamespace="http://www.example.com/some-types">

  <xs:element
      name="EmployeeNumber"
      id="employee_number_type"
      type="xs:integer"/>

</xs:schema>                              (reference)
```

(a) An element declaration, in some schema file `schema.xsd`.

```
<xs:element
    name="AircraftTypeAxis"
    substitutionGroup="xbrldt:dimensionItem"
    abstract="true"
    xbrldt:typedDomainRef="schema.xsd#employee_number_type"

    xbrli:periodType="duration"
    type="xbrli:stringItemType"
    nillable="true">
```

(b) A typed dimension declaration pointing to the above element declaration.

Figure 7.30: A report element declaration which defines the typed dimension `us-gaap:EmployeeNumberAxis`. It has a `xbrldt:typedDomainRef` that carries a URI that points to a complex element declaration elsewhere in the schema.

XML complex types to the end XBRL user, breaking data independence and making interoperability with other syntaxes (JSON, CSV) hard to achieve.

```
<xs:element
    xmlns:xs="http://www.w3.org/2001/XMLSchema"
    xmlns:xbrli="http://www.xbrl.org/2003/instance"

    name="AircraftTypeMember"        Member metadata
    substitutionGroup="xbrli:item"
    type="xbrli:domainItemType"
    abstract="true"

    xbrli:periodType="duration"
    nillable="true"/>
```

Figure 7.31: A report element declaration which defines the member **us-gaap:AircraftTypeMember**. It appears in an XBRL taxonomy schema. We include the prefix bindings, although in practice they are on the root **xbrli:xbrl** element

Member report elements

A member is declared with a syntax very similar to that for concepts and abstracts as well. Figure 7.31 shows the syntax for declaring a dimension.

What characterizes the report element as a member is that its substitution group is **xbrldt:item**, that it is abstract, and that its type should be **xbrli:domainItemType**. The **name** attribute carries the local name of the declared dimension.

It is important to note that, from a specification perspective, a member cannot be distinguished from an abstract, as bearing the type **xbrli:domainItemType**, although encouraged, is not mandatory. If it is known that the taxonomy sticks to the **xbrli:do mainItemType** convention, then it is safe to rely on it. Otherwise, members can be inferred from the definition network because they are in the transitive closure of dimensions. However, this is very cumbersome, and thus encouraged to adhere to the xbrli:domainItemType convention. Finally, in taxonomies such as US-GAAP, the names ending with Member or Domain give a clue as well, even though risky to rely on in software.

The XBRL dimensions specification would not formally disallow any concept or abstract from appearing as a member below a dimension, however this is discouraged and it is paramount to treat members as separate kinds of report elements.

The other attributes are purely syntactic and have either mandatory values, or best practice values:

- the nillable attribute should be set to true.

- the xbrli:periodType attribute should be set to duration.

These attributes have no effect, as members cannot be nilled and have no period types. They are here for modular reasons, as the dimensions specification was introduced later than the core XBRL 2.1 specification.

Finally, even though members carry the xbrli:domainItemType type, this type has a virtual value space, as no facts ever get reported against it.

Line-items report elements

A line-items report element is declared with a syntax very similar to that for concepts and abstracts as well. Figure 7.32 shows the syntax for declaring a dimension.

The name attribute carries the local name of the declared line-items report element. A line-items report element cannot be distinguished from an abstract report element only looking at a taxonomy schema. This is because the notion of line-items report element does not exist in XBRL specifications, and is only established best practice in presentation-oriented taxonomies. Line items can be detected in presentation network because they are the direct

```
<xs:element
    xmlns:xs="http://www.w3.org/2001/XMLSchema"
    xmlns:xbrli="http://www.xbrl.org/2003/instance"
    name="StatementLineItems"          Line-items metadata
    substitutionGroup="xbrli:item"
    abstract="true"

    type="xbrli:stringItemType"
    xbrli:periodType="duration"
    nillable="true"/>
```

Figure 7.32: A line-items declaration which defines the member us-gaap:StatementLineItems. It appears in an XBRL taxonomy schema. We include the prefix bindings, although in practice they are on the root xbrli:xbrl element

children of hypercubes (besides dimensions), and in definition networks on the source side of *all* and *notAll* edges. Finally, in taxonomies such as US-GAAP, the names ending with LineItems give a clue as well, even though risky to rely on in software.

The XBRL specifications, which do not know about these, will not formally disallow any line-items report element to be used elsewhere as a normal abstract or (!) as a member. It will also not disallow a concept from appearing at the top of a line items hierarchy below a hypercube in a presentation network, or even from directly being bound to a hypercube in a definition network. However, it is encouraged to treat line-items report elements separately from abstracts, concepts and members, and to stick to established practice in presentation-based taxonomies.

The other attributes are purely syntactic and have either mandatory values, or best practice values:

- the `nillable` attribute should be set to true.

- the `type` attribute should be set to `xbrli:stringItemType`.

- the `xbrli:periodType` attribute should be set to `duration`.

These attributes have no effect, as members cannot be nilled and have no period types. They are here for modular reasons, as the dimensions specification was introduced later than the core XBRL 2.1 specification.

Finally, even though members carry the `xbrli:domainItemType` type, this type has a virtual value space, as no facts ever get reported against it.

7.10.2 Presentation networks

We do not have much to say on on how presentation networks are affected by the presence of hypercubes and dimensions: the syntax is identical, being aware that this chapter introduced four more report elements that can appear in them. Referencing them with locators is no different than referencing the previously introduced concepts and abstracts.

On the syntactic level, the six kinds of report elements can be assembled in any way, with no constraints. Sticking to the conventions described in this chapter are thus the responsibility, ideally, of the XBRL engine implementor and if not, of the end user.

7.10.3 Label linkbases

Labels are attached to the four new kinds of report elements (hypercubes, dimensions, members, line-items report elements) in the same way as they are for concepts and abstracts: one can define labels in different languages, define labels that document report elements with the appropriate label roles, and so on.

Of course, as is the case for abstracts, common sense dictates that some label roles do not make sense for report elements that are not concepts: negative labels, total labels, and the like, have no point being used with a hypercube, a dimension or a member.

7.10.4 Definition networks

We now introduce the syntax of definition networks, starting with good news: most of it looks exactly like the syntax of presentation, calculation and label networks. What we need to introduce here are the names of the linkbase elements, the names of the arcs, and the arc roles.

Definition linkbase element

The root of a definition linkbase is `link:definitionLink`. This fits together with the other linkbase elements: `link:presentati onLink`, `link:calculationLink`, `link:labelLink`

Nodes

The nodes of definition networks are all locators, as is the case in presentation and calculation networks. These locators can reference any of the six kinds of report elements, and the syntax is identical to how concepts and abstracts are referenced.

Edges

The name of the edge elements, also called arcs, in a definition network, is `link:definitionArc`. Edges connect nodes with the same attributes `xlink:from` and `xlink:to`, referring to the `xlink:label` values of the locators. The `xlink:type` is also set to "arc", like edges in any other linkbase.

What is different in a definition linkbase is the usage of arc roles. In a presentation linkbase, all arc roles are identical, and the same is true for calculation linkbases and label linkbases. However, definition linkbases carry hypercube validation syntax using several types of arc roles, summarized on Figure 7.33[28].

Arc roles must be chosen depending on the source and target report elements. For example, a hypercube must be connected to a dimension with the `hypercube-dimension` arc role. For example, a dimension must be connected to a member with the `dimension-domain` arc role.

Figures 7.34 and 7.35 show the syntax corresponding to the definition network previously shown on Figure 7.21. As the reader can see, although definition linkbases, like other linkbases, can be lengthy and look complex, they are nothing else than a boring list of locators and arcs.

---

[28]The core XBRL specification also defines four more arc roles: `general-special`, `essence-alias`, `similar-tuple`, `requires-element`. They have nothing to do with hypercubes and have more of an ontological aspect. They are left outside of the scope of this book, as they are not commonly used in practice.

Arc role	Semantics and use
http://xbrl.org/int/dim/arcrole/all	from a line-items report element to a (positive) hypercube
http://xbrl.org/int/dim/arcrole/notAll	from a line-items report element to a (negative) hypercube
http://xbrl.org/int/dim/arcrole/hypercube-dimension	from a hypercube to a dimension
http://xbrl.org/int/dim/arcrole/dimension-default	from a dimension to its default member (usually a domain)
http://xbrl.org/int/dim/arcrole/dimension-domain	from dimension to its top-level member (the domain)
http://xbrl.org/int/dim/arcrole/domain-member	from a member (which can be a domain) to another member below a dimension or between line-items report elements, abstracts and concepts in the line items hierarchy.

Figure 7.33: The arc roles used in a definition network. The arc roles all and notAll are also commonly called has-hypercube.

```
<?xml version="1.0"?>
<link:linkbase
    xmlns:link="http://www.xbrl.org/2003/linkbase"
    xmlns:xlink="http://www.w3.org/1999/xlink"
    xsi:schemaLocation="
      http://www.xbrl.org/2003/linkbase
      http://www.xbrl.org/2003/xbrl-linkbase-2003-12-31.xsd
      ">

    <link:definitionLink xlink:type="extended"
        xlink:role="http://www.xbrl.org/2003/role/link">
      <link:loc xlink:type="locator"
        xlink:href="taxonomy.xsd#DirectorsCompensationLineItems"
        xlink:label="sample_DirectorsCompensationLineItems"/>
      <link:definitionArc xlink:type="arc"
        xlink:from="sample_DirectorsCompensationLineItems"
        xlink:to="sample_DirectorsCompensationTable"
        xlink:arcrole="http://xbrl.org/int/dim/arcrole/all"
        xbrldt:closed="true"
        xbrldt:contextElementType="segment"/>
      <link:loc xlink:type="locator"
        xlink:href="taxonomy.xsd#DirectorsCompensationTable"
        xlink:label="sample_DirectorsCompensationTable"/>
      <link:definitionArc xlink:type="arc"
        xlink:from="sample_DirectorsCompensationTable"
        xlink:to="sample_DirectorAxis"
        xlink:arcrole="http://xbrl.org/int/dim/arcrole/hypercube-dimension"/>
      <link:loc xlink:type="locator"
        xlink:href="taxonomy.xsd#DirectorAxis"
        xlink:label="sample_DirectorAxis"/>
      <link:definitionArc xlink:type="arc"
        xlink:from="sample_DirectorAxis"
        xlink:to="sample_DirectorDomain"
        xlink:arcrole="http://xbrl.org/int/dim/arcrole/dimension-domain"/>
      <link:loc xlink:type="locator"
        xlink:href="taxonomy.xsd#DirectorDomain"
        xlink:label="sample_DirectorDomain"/>
      <link:definitionArc xlink:type="arc"
        xlink:from="sample_DirectorAxis"
        xlink:to="sample_DirectorDomain"
        xlink:arcrole="http://xbrl.org/int/dim/arcrole/dimension-default"/>
      <link:definitionArc xlink:type="arc"
        xlink:from="sample_DirectorDomain"
        xlink:to="sample_JohnDoeMember"
        xlink:arcrole="http://xbrl.org/int/dim/arcrole/domain-member"/>
      <link:loc xlink:type="locator"
        xlink:href="taxonomy.xsd#JohnDoeMember"
        xlink:label="sample_JohnDoeMember"/>
      <link:definitionArc xlink:type="arc"
        xlink:from="sample_DirectorDomain"
        xlink:to="sample_JaneDoeMember"
        xlink:arcrole="http://xbrl.org/int/dim/arcrole/domain-member"/>
      <link:loc xlink:type="locator"
        xlink:href="taxonomy.xsd#JaneDoeMember"
        xlink:label="sample_JaneDoeMember"/>
```

Figure 7.34: The syntax of a complete definition network, in a linkbase. Each definition network uses an extended link `link:definitionLink`. We assume that the report elements are all defined in a schema called taxonomy.xsd, with user-friendly IDs.

```
    <link:definitionArc xlink:type="arc"
      xlink:from="sample_DirectorsCompensationLineItems"
      xlink:to="sample_DirectorsCompensationHierarchy"
      xlink:arcrole="http://xbrl.org/int/dim/arcrole/domain-member"/>
    <link:loc xlink:type="locator"
      xlink:href="taxonomy.xsd#DirectorsCompensationHierarchy"
      xlink:label="sample_DirectorsCompensationHierarchy"/>
    <link:definitionArc xlink:type="arc"
      xlink:from="DirectorsCompensationHierarchy"
      xlink:to="sample_DirectorSalary"
      xlink:arcrole="http://xbrl.org/int/dim/arcrole/domain-member"/>
    <link:loc xlink:type="locator"
      xlink:href="taxonomy.xsd#sample_DirectorSalary"
      xlink:label="sample_sample_DirectorSalary"/>
    <link:definitionArc xlink:type="arc"
      xlink:from="DirectorsCompensationHierarchy"
      xlink:to="sample_DirectorBonus"
      xlink:arcrole="http://xbrl.org/int/dim/arcrole/domain-member"/>
    <link:loc xlink:type="locator"
      xlink:href="taxonomy.xsd#sample_DirectorBonus"
      xlink:label="sample_DirectorBonus"/>
    <link:definitionArc xlink:type="arc"
      xlink:from="DirectorsCompensationHierarchy"
      xlink:to="sample_DirectorFee"
      xlink:arcrole="http://xbrl.org/int/dim/arcrole/domain-member"/>
    <link:loc xlink:type="locator"
      xlink:href="taxonomy.xsd#sample_DirectorFee"
      xlink:label="sample_DirectorFee"/>
    <link:definitionArc xlink:type="arc"
      xlink:from="DirectorsCompensationHierarchy"
      xlink:to="sample_DirectorOptionsGrantedAtFairValue"
      xlink:arcrole="http://xbrl.org/int/dim/arcrole/domain-member"/>
    <link:loc xlink:type="locator"
      xlink:href="taxonomy.xsd#sample_DirectorFee"
      xlink:label="sample_DirectorOptionsGrantedAtFairValue"/>
  </link:definitionLink>

</link:linkbase>
```

Figure 7.35: The syntax of a complete definition network, continued

Context element type

The attribute `xbrldt:contextElementType`, which is mandatory on edges with the arc role `all` or `notAll`, specifies where in the instance dimension values are to be stored. Its value is called a container and is either "segment" or "scenario". How the instance looks like depending on this value is shown in Section 7.10.5.

For filings to the SEC, the Edgar Filer Manual specifies that only segment containers must be used.

Open and closed hypercubes

Hypercubes can be closed by associating the attribute `xbrldt:closed` with the value true on the `all` or `notAll` arc. If this attribute is absent, or has the value `open`, then the hypercube is considered to be open.

Typed dimensions

Typed dimensions can be associated with a hypercube, but cannot be the source of a `dimension-member` arc, as their domain is already defined by means of the `xbrldt:typedDomainRef` in the taxonomy schema.

Target roles and modularity

Edges in a definition network can carry an `xbrldt:targetRole` attribute that contains the network identifier URI of a different network. The semantics of this modularity were explained in Section 7.6.9.

7.10.5 Instances using dimensions

Now that we have seen the syntax for introducing hypercube validation in taxonomies, that is, for the four newly introduced report elements and definition linkbases, let us go back to the instance that reports facts against the taxonomy.

We have introduced the general syntax of an instance in Section 2.8. In particular, we have seen that the values associated with the entity and period aspects are stored in a syntactic `context`. The values associated with dimensions, that is, members if the dimension is explicit or typed values if the dimension is typed, are also stored in the syntactic `xbrli:context`.

There are two places in the `xbrli:context` where the user-defined dimensional coordinates of the fact can be stored: the segment (`xbrli:segment`), nested inside the `xbrli:entity`, or the `xbrli:scenario`. Which one applies is decided in the definition linkbase on the edge that associates the line items hierarchy with a hypercube, by means of the attribute `xbrldt:contextElement Type`.

Explicit dimensions

We start with explicit dimensions. Figure 7.36 shows a fact that is valid against Charles Hoffmann's Director Compensation definition network previously shown in Figure 7.21. Dimensions, in this example, are stored in the `xbrli:segment`, assuming the definition linkbase says so. The `xbrli:segment` element contains an unordered list of children `xbrldi:explicitMember` elements.

`xbrldi:explicitMember` elements have:

- an attribute dimension that is associated with the SQName of a dimension,

- and simple content that contains the SQName of the associated member in the case of an explicit dimension.

It is recommended to follow this common practice in other taxonomies as well, even though there would be no semantic difference using `xbrli:scenario` instead.

```xml
<?xml version="1.0"?>
<xbrli:xbrl
    xmlns:xbrli="http://www.xbrl.org/2003/instance"
    xmlns:xbrldi="http://xbrl.org/2006/xbrldi"
    xmlns:pattern=
        "http://www.xbrlsite.com/DigitalFinancialReporting/Metapattern/MadeUp"
    xmlns:ISO4217="http://www.xbrl.org/2003/iso4217">

  <xbrli:context id="john-doe-in-2017">

    <xbrli:entity>
      <xbrli:identifier scheme="http://www.sec.gov/CIK">
        1234567890 <!-- A hypothetical CIK for a sample company -->
      </xbrli:identifier>
      <xbrli:segment>
        <xbrldi:explicitMember dimension="pattern:DirectorAxis">
          pattern:JohnDoeMember
        </xbrldi:explicitMember>             Dimension metadata
      </xbrli:segment>
    </xbrli:entity>

    <xbrli:period>
      <xbrli:duration>
        <xbrli:startDate>2017-01-01</xbrli:startDate>
        <xbrli:endDate>2017-12-31</xbrli:endDate>
      </xbrli:instant>
    </xbrli:period>

  </xbrli:context>

  <xbrli:unit id="dollars">
    <xbrli:measure>
      ISO4217:USD
    </xbrli:measure>
  </xbrli:unit>

  <sample:DirectorSalary
      contextRef="john-doe-in-2017"
      unitRef="dollars"
      decimals="-6">
    1000
  </sample:DirectorSalary>

</xbrli:xbrl>
```

Figure 7.36: An XBRL instance reporting a fact that carries dimensions in its context, using the segment container.

Figure 7.37 shows the same fact, but using the `xbrli:scenario` container instead. The layout inside this container is identical. In the case that the `xbrli:scenario` container is used instead of `xbrli:segment`[29], it is recommended to stick to it, that is, not spread dimension-value pairs across these two containers.

---

[29]so, against SEC practice

```
<?xml version="1.0"?>
<xbrli:xbrl
    xmlns:xbrli="http://www.xbrl.org/2003/instance"
    xmlns:xbrldi="http://xbrl.org/2006/xbrldi"
    xmlns:pattern=
        "http://www.xbrlsite.com/DigitalFinancialReporting/Metapattern/MadeUp"
    xmlns:ISO4217="http://www.xbrl.org/2003/iso4217">

    <xbrli:context id="john-doe-in-2017">

        <xbrli:entity>
            <xbrli:identifier scheme="http://www.sec.gov/CIK">
                1234567890 <!-- A hypothetical CIK for a sample company -->
            </xbrli:identifier>
        </xbrli:entity>

        <xbrli:period>
            <xbrli:duration>
                <xbrli:startDate>2017-01-01</xbrli:startDate>
                <xbrli:endDate>2017-12-31</xbrli:endDate>
            </xbrli:instant>
        </xbrli:period>
        <xbrli:scenario>
            <xbrldi:explicitMember dimension="pattern:DirectorAxis">
                pattern:JohnDoeMember
            </xbrldi:explicitMember>
            <xbrldi:explicitMember dimension="pattern:SubsidiaryAxis">
                pattern:GermanyBranchMember
            </xbrldi:explicitMember>                    Dimension metadata
        </xbrli:scenario>

    </xbrli:context>

    <xbrli:unit id="dollars">
        <xbrli:measure>
            ISO4217:USD
        </xbrli:measure>
    </xbrli:unit>

    <sample:DirectorSalary
        contextRef="john-doe-in-2017"
        unitRef="dollars"
        decimals="-6">
        1000
    </sample:DirectorSalary>

</xbrli:xbrl>
```

Figure 7.37: An XBRL instance reporting a fact that carries dimensions in its context, using the scenario container. We added a dimension for the sake of showing that several dimension-member pairs can be present in this container.

Typed dimensions

Typed dimension values also appear in either the xbrli:segment
or xbrli:segment container, depending on what the linkbase says
for the associated dimension. A typed dimension is associated with
a value using the xbrldi:typedMember element. Its dimension
attribute specifies the SQName of the dimension, and its content
carries the value. Figure 7.38 shows an example.

The value must be valid against the type of the dimension.
From a syntactic viewpoint, this value is an XML element, and its
type is the XML element type associated with the dimension in the
definition linkbase. However, as explained earlier in this chapter,
typed dimensions should normally only involve simple types as is
XBRL best practice, meaning that the XML element under xbrl
di:typedMember will typically carry an atomic value, such as a
string, an integer or a date, and its name, defined in the schema,
is irrelevant to the end user.

```
<?xml version="1.0"?>
<xbrli:xbrl
    xmlns:xbrli="http://www.xbrl.org/2003/instance"
    xmlns:xbrldi="http://xbrl.org/2006/xbrldi"
    xmlns:pattern=
        "http://www.xbrlsite.com/DigitalFinancialReporting/Metapattern/MadeUp"
    xmlns:ISO4217="http://www.xbrl.org/2003/iso4217">

  <xbrli:context id="john-doe-in-2017">

    <xbrli:entity>
      <xbrli:identifier scheme="http://www.sec.gov/CIK">
        1234567890 <!-- A hypothetical CIK for a sample company -->
      </xbrli:identifier>
      <xbrli:segment>
        <xbrldi:explicitMember dimension="pattern:DirectorAxis">
          pattern:JaneDoeMember
        </xbrldi:explicitMember>
        <xbrldi:typedMember dimension="pattern:EmployeeCodeAxis">
          <code>123456</code>                 Typed dimension and its value
        </xbrldi:typedMember>
      </xbrli:segment>

    </xbrli:entity>

    <xbrli:period>
      <xbrli:duration>
        <xbrli:startDate>2017-01-01</xbrli:startDate>
        <xbrli:endDate>2017-12-31</xbrli:endDate>
      </xbrli:instant>
    </xbrli:period>

  </xbrli:context>

  <xbrli:unit id="dollars">
    <xbrli:measure>
      ISO4217:USD
    </xbrli:measure>
  </xbrli:unit>

  <sample:DirectorSalary
      contextRef="john-doe-in-2017"
      unitRef="dollars"
      decimals="-6">
    1000
  </sample:DirectorSalary>

</xbrli:xbrl>
```

Figure 7.38: An XBRL instance reporting a fact that carries a typed dimension (the employee number), in this case in a segment container. Here, the dimension has the type integer, and the value is carried by the **code** element, the name of which is irrelevant semantically but is decided in the schema.

Chapter 8

Reference

This chapter provides further references to namespaces, label roles, links and, ultimately, to the specifications underlying the XBRL standard.

8.1   Vocabulary

Abstract This is one of the six kinds of report elements. An abstract helps organizing and structuring concepts in a presentation hierarchy. Facts cannot report values against abstracts. Unlike in this book, in XBRL specifications, syntactic abstracts correspond to any element declaration that is abstract, which includes all report elements (dimensions, hypercubes, members, ...) except concepts. We advise refraining from using the word abstract in this way.

Aspect an aspect acts as a dimension along which facts can be organized in cubes. It is associated with a value. Aspects can be builtin (concept, period, entity, unit, language) or user-defined (XBRL dimensions).

243

Base set this is terminology used in XBRL specifications. A base set is a subset of the DTS linkbase made of edges that share the same link name, linkrole, arc name and arcrole. Base sets are used to define the semantics of taxonomy extension and overriding.

Concept this is one of the five builtin aspects and also one of the six kinds of report elements. The concept of a fact says *what* the value of a fact is (Assets, Income, etc.). Unlike in this book, in XBRL specifications, syntactic concepts correspond to element declarations used to define items and may thus also be abstract elements (thus any report elements, not only concept report elements) and tuples. We advise refraining from using the word concept in this way.

Calculation linkbase this is a subgraph of the DTS linkbase that organize concepts to express simple calculation-based relationships, such as EquityAndLiabilities = Equity + Liabilities. The intersection of the calculation linkbasewith a network is called a calculation network.

Component This is a meaningful cube of data. A component is identified by a network and a hypercube and can contain a presentation network, a calculation network, a definition network.

Context a set of aspect/value pairs that gives a semantic context to a fact. Unlike in this book, in XBRL specifications, syntactic contexts do not include concepts and units.

Definition linkbase this is a subgraph of the DTS linkbase that organize report elements to express hypercube validation rules. The intersection of the definition linkbasewith a network is called a definition network. Note that definition network also support other standard arcs such as essence-alias, same-tuple, general-special and requires-element.

Dimension this is a user-defined aspect. A dimension can be either explicit, in which the context of a fact associates it with a member, or typed, in which case it is associated with an atomic value such as an integer or a date.

Discoverable Taxonomy Set this is the set of all XBRL metadata associated with an instance. The DTS contains a taxonomy schema and a linkbase. The DTS is discovered and built by following pointers to a DAG of XML and XML Schema files on the syntactic level.

Domain this is a special kind of member that appears at the top of a member hierarchy. Often, a domain has aggregating semantics and also acts as the default value of a dimension.

Entity this is one of the five builtin aspects. The entity of a facts says *to whom* the value of a fact applies. Very often, the entity is also the reporting entity which files the report.

Fact an atom of reported data. It is a value, normally atomic (but which can be a big chunk of text), associated with a context. If the value is a number, it may also carry a precision.

Hypercube This is one of the six kinds of report elements. Hypercubes organize facts in cubes thanks to a set of dimensions and their member hierarchies. A hypercube only makes sense in a network, as hypercube names can be reused across networks.

Item this is terminology used in XBRL specifications. An item corresponds to a report element.

Label linkbase this is a subgraph of the DTS linkbase that associates report elements to user-friendly labels. The label linkbase is usually organized as a single, default network as labels apply throughout the DTS.

Line-items report element This is one of the six kinds of report elements. A line-items report element appears at the top of a hierarchy of concepts and abstracts.

Linkbase A linkbase is a graph of report elements and resources (such as labels). Edges in a linkbase carry information (link names, linkroles, arc names, arcroles). If this word is used alone, the linkbase is the entire graph contained in a DTS.

Member this is a value that can be associated with an explicit dimension. Members are organized in hierarchies in a definition network.

Network A network is a subset of the entire linkbase that groups facts in a semantically meaningful unit, such as the balance sheet network, the income statement network, etc. Syntactically, a network identifier is a linkrole URI.

Period this is one of the five builtin aspects. The period of a fact says *when* the value of a fact applies. It can be an instant period or a duration, or be forever.

Presentation linkbase this is a subgraph of the DTS linkbase that organize report elements for user-friendly display. The intersection of the presentation linkbasewith a network is called a presentation network.

Primary item this is terminology used in XBRL specifications. A primary item corresponds to a concept, abstract, member or line-items report element and thus hypercubes and dimensions are not primary items.

Unit this is one of the five builtin aspects. The unit of a fact says *in what* the value of a fact is expressed. The most widely used units are currencies with codes following the ISO4217 standard, but the standard unit registry also supports physical units such as units of lengths, of mass, etc.

Tuple tuples are a syntactic construct that allows grouping and organizing facts in trees. It is recommended, however, to use hypercubes and definition linkbases instead.

8.2 Namespaces

Figure 8.1 summarizes the prefix bindings and namespaces commonly used in the industry, and used throughout this book. Although prefixes are irrelevant and only namespaces matter, we very highly recommend to stick to these prefixes for interoperability and readability.

Prefix	Namespace	Use
xml	http://www.w3.org/XML/1998/namespace	Standard XML namespace, used for languages
xlink	http://www.w3.org/1999/xlink	XML Link (underlying standard)
xs	http://www.w3.org/2001/XMLSchema	XML Schema, used in taxonomy schemata
xsi	http://www.w3.org/2001/XMLSchema-instance	used for linking instances to XML Schemata
xbrli	http://www.xbrl.org/2003/instance	used in XBRL instances, also in taxonomy schemas
xbrldi	http://xbrl.org/2006/xbrldi	used in instances that leverage dimensions
xbrldt	http://xbrl.org/2005/xbrldt	used in taxonomy schemas that leverage dimensions, and in definition linkbases
link	http://www.xbrl.org/2003/linkbase	used in linkbases
xl	http://www.xbrl.org/2003/XLink	used internally in specifications
ISO4217	http://www.xbrl.org/2003/iso4217	for currency codes
utr	http://www.xbrl.org/2009/utr	for additionally standardized units
nonnum	http://www.xbrl.org/dtr/type/non-numeric	for additionally standardized non-numeric types
num	http://www.xbrl.org/dtr/type/numeric	for additionally standardized numeric types

Figure 8.1: Namespaces and prefixes commonly used in practice.

8.3 Link names, arc names, arcroles

Figure 8.2 lists the standard link names, arc names and arc roles commonly encountered in XBRL and explained in this book. The last five rows also include a few definition and reference arcroles not (yet) documented in this book. We also do not cover here generic labels and generic links, which are used for defining table linkbases.

Technically, for each row in this table and for each possible link role (network identifier), we get a presentation network, calculation network, etc. However, in the case of XBRL dimensions, the five arcroles (all, notAll, hypercube-dimension, dimension-domain, domain-member) only make sense taken together for hypercube validation, which is why we abuse the terminology and, in this book, consider them as a single definition network.

Type of linkbase	Link name	Arc name	Arc role
Label	link:labelLink	link:labelArc	http://www.xbrl.org/2003/arcrole/concept-label
Presentation	link:presentationLink	link:presentationArc	http://www.xbrl.org/2003/arcrole/parent-child
Calculation	link:calculationLink	link:calculationArc	http://www.xbrl.org/2003/arcrole/summation-item
Definition	link:definitionLink	link:definitionArc	http://www.xbrl.org/int/dim/arcrole/all
Definition	link:definitionLink	link:definitionArc	http://www.xbrl.org/int/dim/arcrole/notAll
Definition	link:definitionLink	link:definitionArc	http://www.xbrl.org/int/dim/arcrole/hypercube-dimension
Definition	link:definitionLink	link:definitionArc	http://www.xbrl.org/int/dim/arcrole/dimension-domain
Definition	link:definitionLink	link:definitionArc	http://www.xbrl.org/int/dim/arcrole/domain-member
Definition	link:definitionLink	link:definitionArc	http://www.xbrl.org/2003/arcrole/general-special
Definition	link:definitionLink	link:definitionArc	http://www.xbrl.org/2003/arcrole/essence-alias
Definition	link:definitionLink	link:definitionArc	http://www.xbrl.org/2003/arcrole/similar-tuples
Definition	link:definitionLink	link:definitionArc	http://www.xbrl.org/2003/arcrole/requires-element
Reference	link:referenceLink	link:referenceArc	http://www.xbrl.org/2003/arcrole/concept-reference

Figure 8.2: Standardized label roles used in presentation.

8.4 Label roles

Figure 8.3 summarizes all standardized label roles that can be used in presentation networks. Figure 8.4 summarizes all standardized label roles that are not used in presentation networks, but that contain documentation on the concept and its usage.

Label role URI	Use
http://www.xbrl.org/2003/role/label	standard label (can be omitted)
http://www.xbrl.org/2003/role/terseLabel	less verbosity
http://www.xbrl.org/2003/role/verboseLabel	more verbosity
http://www.xbrl.org/2003/role/positiveLabel	presenting a positive value
http://www.xbrl.org/2003/role/positiveTerseLabel	presenting a positive value (less verbose)
http://www.xbrl.org/2003/role/positiveVerboseLabel	presenting a positive value (more verbose)
http://www.xbrl.org/2003/role/negativeLabel	presenting a negative value
http://www.xbrl.org/2003/role/negativeTerseLabel	presenting a negative value (less verbose)
http://www.xbrl.org/2003/role/negativeVerboseLabel	presenting a negative value (more verbose)
http://www.xbrl.org/2003/role/zeroLabel	presenting a zero value
http://www.xbrl.org/2003/role/zeroTerseLabel	presenting a zero value (less verbose)
http://www.xbrl.org/2003/role/zeroVerboseLabel	presenting a zero value (more verbose)
http://www.xbrl.org/2003/role/totalLabel	presenting a total
http://www.xbrl.org/2003/role/periodStartLabel	presenting an instance value as starting a period
http://www.xbrl.org/2003/role/periodEndLabel	presenting an instance value as ending a period

Figure 8.3: Standardized label roles used in presentation.

Label role URI	Use
http://www.xbrl.org/2003/role/documentation	documents the concept
http://www.xbrl.org/2003/role/definitionGuidance	defines the concept
http://www.xbrl.org/2003/role/disclosureGuidance	indicates how desirable it is that the concept be reported
http://www.xbrl.org/2003/role/presentationGuidance	provides guidance on presentation
http://www.xbrl.org/2003/role/measurementGuidance	provides guidance on measurement of values
http://www.xbrl.org/2003/role/commentaryGuidance	some further comments can be put in here
http://www.xbrl.org/2003/role/exampleGuidance	provides an example

Figure 8.4: Standardized label roles used only for documentation purposes (not for presentation).

8.5   XBRL specifications

A book is usually the best way to get an introduction to a new technology or to learn it while specifications are more intended to be used, and followed, by compliant implementers or vendors.

However, a book cannot cover as much ground as a complete set of specifications, which is why they exist, so that the latter remain the ideal place to look at in case of any doubts regarding details, even for users. The language is of course more technical and a bit harder to read before going to bed, but once one is familiar with their overall structure, it becomes increasingly easy to quickly get answers to specific questions.

We summarize here pointers to the specifications underlying XBRL. They are the ultimate reference for clarifying small and specific details, as well as for implementers of XBRL products.

8.5.1   Core XBRL specification

The core XBRL specification introduces facts, taxonomy schemata as well as the definition, calculation, presentation, label and reference linkbases. The current version is XBRL 2.1.

```
http://specifications.xbrl.org/work-product-index-gro
up-base-spec-base-spec.html
```

8.5.2   XBRL Dimensions specification

The XBRL dimensions specification introduces hypercubes, dimensions, hypercube validation, and the appropriate new edges (all, notAll, hypercube-dimension, dimension-domain, domain-member) in definition linkbases. The current version is XBRL Dimension 1.0.

```
https://specifications.xbrl.org/spec-group-index-gro
up-dimensions.html
```

8.5.3 XBRL Formula: Variables specification

The XBRL Variables specification introduces is part of a bigger framework not covered yet in this edition: XBRL Formula. However, this specification is interesting, because it introduces an aspect model on which the XBRL data model is based. The current version is XBRL Variables 1.0.

http://www.xbrl.org/specification/variables/rec-2009-06-22/
variables-rec-2009-06-22+corrected-errata-2013-11-18.ht
ml

8.5.4 Data type registry

The data type registry as well as the underlying specifications on the process and structure are available here:

http://specifications.xbrl.org/work-product-index-reg
istries-dtr-1.0.html

8.5.5 Units registry

The units registry as well as the underlying specifications on the process and structure are available here:

http://specifications.xbrl.org/work-product-index-reg
istries-units-registry-1.0.html

8.5.6 Open information model

The Open Information Model, currently a Candidate Recommendation, provides an abstract view over the data model underlying facts, as well as alternate JSON and CSV syntaxes. This goes in the (right) direction of disconnecting the XBRL data model from XML. Note that may be a few small discrepancies between the OIM and the XBRL Variables specification, as there are competing opinions on certain aspects of the XBRL data model.

```
http://specifications.xbrl.org/work-product-index-ope
n-information-model-open-information-model.html
```

Table Linkbase

Table linkbases, which are central to the user-friendly display of
instances tied with DPM-based taxonomies, are not (yet) covered
in this edition, even though all fancy renderings used across this
book follow similar conventions (L-shapes, etc). We provide a link
for further reference.

```
https://specifications.xbrl.org/spec-group-index-tab
le-linkbase.html
```

8.6   Regulator specific documents

8.6.1   Edgar Filer Manual (presentation-based reports)

The SEC provides a set of additional rules that XBRL instances
(10-Q, 10-K, etc.) submitted to them via Edgar must fulfil. Many
of these rules are used by other regulatory authorities as well,
and some of them are also practices recommended throughout this
book. Part 6 of Volume 2 is especially interesting.

```
https://www.sec.gov/info/edgar/edgarfm-vol2-v42.pdf
```

8.6.2   European Banking Authority architecture (DPM-based reports)

The EBA published the DPM architecture under the following link.

```
https://www.eba.europa.eu/documents/10180/632822/EBA+
Architecture+for+XBRL+representation+of+DPM.pdf
```

8.7 XML specifications

XML

The core XML specification lays the groundwork for the XML syntax. XML instances, XML taxonomy schemata and XML taxonomy linkbases are all special cases of XML documents. This is version 1.0 and there is a newer version 1.1 that mostly introduces internationalization and otherwise does not change much. XML 1.0 is however still widely in use.

https://www.w3.org/TR/REC-xml/

8.7.1 XML Names

The "Namespaces in XML" specification introduces namespaces in XML names, as well as prefixes and bindings from prefixes to namespaces.

https://www.w3.org/TR/xml-names/

8.7.2 XML Schema

The XML Schema specification specifies how XML itself can be used to validate XML documents. XBRL taxonomy schemata are XML schema documents. We point to version 1.0, but here to there is a new version 1.1 available.

https://www.w3.org/TR/xmlschema-0/

8.7.3 XML Link

The XML Link specification specifies simple and extended links can be defined. `schemaRef`, `linkbaseRef`, `roleRef`, `arcroleRef` are all simple links. XML taxonomy linkbases are also linkbases, and contain extended links, in the sense of the XML Link specification.

https://www.w3.org/TR/xlink11/

Chapter 9

Not covered

XBRL has a very vast scope, and for this first edition, we made the choice of covering the basics with the goal of getting started with XBRL. In particular, the following aspects of XBRL are not covered in this first edition, but may be introduced in subsequent editions:

- Footnotes, which are linkbases that associate facts with footnotes

- References, which allow concepts to point to reference information such as accounting codes or standardized shortcuts.

- Tuples, which group concepts, and facts, together. However, tuples are nowadays considered obsolete by many authorities, having been superseded by hypercube structures.

- JSON syntax, Open Information Model (OIM). As explained in this book, XBRL is not XML. Recently a working group in XBRL International has started an attempt to standardize XBRL's data model and extend it with further syntaxes such as JSON. The data model explained in this book is compatible with the OIM in spirit; we actually welcomed the OIM initiative with open arms, as it brings XBRL in the right direction.

- Formulas, Variables, Filters (including further patterns such as roll forwards). This is a generalization of calculation networks to support more arbitrary business rules and patterns.

- Table linkbases. This is a standardization of user-facing interfaces for viewing or editing XBRL reports. Reports can also specify their own interfaces, which is very actively used by some regulatory authorities such as in the European Union.

List of Figures

Index

CPSIA information can be obtained
at www.ICGtesting.com
Printed in the USA
FSHW04n1936170418
47128FS